Finnish Neutrality

Finnish Neutrality

A Study of Finnish Foreign Policy Since the Second World War

Max Jakobson

HUGH EVELYN LONDON

First Published in 1968 by
Hugh Evelyn Limited,
9 Fitzroy Square,
London, W.1.
© 1968, Max Jakobson
Printed in Great Britain by
R. & R. Clark Limited.
SBN 238.78818.0.

Contents

To Marilyn

Illustrations

Preface

This book falls far short of being a comprehensive history of Finland's foreign policy. The sources for such a work are not yet available. It is rather a collection of sketches and essays on some of the situations and problems Finland has had to deal with since the end of the Second World War. A chapter on Finnish foreign policy from 1917 to 1944 has been included for background.

Several friends and colleagues have helped me with valuable suggestions and comments. I wish to thank them all.

New York, 2nd October 1968
M. J.

1. *The Rebellious Pawn*

THE SMALLER STATES OF EUROPE ARE OFTEN REGARDED AS mere pawns on the chessboard of international politics: objects of Great Power policies rather than masters of their own fate. If this were true, there would be little point in writing about the foreign policy of a small state like Finland; it would be more sensible to describe Finland's international position by writing about the policies of Russia and Germany. But the reality of international relations is more complex, and less predictable or orderly, than the popular analogy with chess implies. By the rules of the game the Finnish pawn ought to have been swept off the board long ago. Yet Finland, born out of the First World War, survived the Second and has lived and prospered through the tensions that have followed it. True, the Finns have usually had no more than marginal control over the external circumstances of their country; their freedom of choice in foreign policy more often than not has been freedom to choose between two evils. But ultimately it has been their own decisions, not decisions imposed by others, that have determined their fate. Just as in shooting a rapid in order to steer one must keep rowing, however futile or even absurd that may seem to someone watching from the shore, so have the Finns kept control over their own affairs, even at times when the current of events may have seemed irresistible. And they have been prudent enough not to attempt to steer upstream, at least not for too long.

Prudence is not among the traits usually ascribed to the Finnish people. The image of Finland that continues to prevail in the Western world was formed in the heroic days of the Winter War of 1939–40, when for a hundred days the Finns held the centre of the world stage. Ever since then they have lived virtually incognito among the nations of Europe, emerging only occasionally and for brief moments above the horizon of international news media. This is in a sense a measure of the success of Finland's policy of keeping out of trouble. But also it has created a gap between the traditional image and contemporary reality.

I

Finland today claims to be a neutral country, yet faithful to a pact of mutual assistance with the Soviet Union; a Western democracy, yet living in friendship with its powerful Communist neighbour. Some foreign observers regard this claim with scepticism: it looks to them like the Indian rope trick – a clever thing to do but not quite believable. Some others, believing it, look upon Finland as a deserter from the front line of the cold war. Others again look beyond Finland for an explanation of the mystery. When, in October 1961, I was in Washington to take part in preparations for President Urho Kekkonen's visit to the United States, I was questioned by the late President John F. Kennedy on various aspects of Finnish policy, but what he really wanted to know was something about Soviet policy. 'What puzzles us Americans', he said, 'is why the Soviet Union has allowed Finland to retain her independence?' This is indeed the question that seems to puzzle many people. But it is based on premises of questionable validity. It implies that in the natural scheme of things the Soviet Union surely must have wished to destroy Finnish independence, and if it has not done so, this must be entirely due to some mysterious calculation on the part of the Soviet leaders – most likely something designed to confuse and deceive the West. That the Finns themselves might have had something to do with maintaining their independence is usually dismissed.

The mystery arises, I believe, not from what actually has happened in Finland, but from the attempt to relate it to a general theory of what ought to have happened. George Kennan writes in his Memoirs about 'the persistent urge [of Americans] to seek universal formulae or doctrines', about 'the tendency to divide the world neatly into Communist and free world components' rather than discriminate and recognize the specific characteristics of each country.[1] The inclination to generalize, the search for categories, is not confined to Americans. It is a universal human failing. Finland is one of its victims. The mystery about Finland resolves itself when developments in Finland are examined against the background of her own unique experiences and circumstances, not those of other countries with which Finland has never had much in common. The question to ask is not why the course of events in Finland has not been different from what it has been, but rather what forces and influences have in fact shaped it, including what the Finns themselves have done about it.

II. Facts of Power: 1917–1944

THE BEGINNING OF FINLAND'S FOREIGN POLICY IN A FORMAL
sense was the declaration of independence on 6th December 1917. In
fact, however, the Finns had managed their relations with other
nations with varying degrees of independence for centuries before
the attainment of full sovereignty.[1]

Even during the time Finland was a province of the Kingdom of
Sweden a distinctly Finnish foreign policy, designed to further Finnish interests rather than those of the Kingdom as a whole, can be
traced in the words and actions of Finnish leaders. Their chief
means of pursuing such interests was to try to influence the policy of
the King and his government; but in some cases they took separate
action in relation to foreign powers; and towards the end of the
eighteenth century some of them began to plan for national independence.

In 1809 the first stage on the road to independence was reached.
Finland was conquered by Russian troops and detached from
Sweden. Tsar Alexander I, in order to gain their allegiance, granted
the Finns far-reaching autonomy. In his words, Finland was 'elevated
as a nation to the ranks of nations'. Naturally he did not mean to
grant his new Grand Duchy autonomy in foreign affairs, but internal autonomy led to the creation of the political institutions as well
as the sense of national identity that were needed for the conduct
of an independent foreign policy.

The Grand Duchy had her own laws and legislature, her own civil
service and judiciary, her own currency and customs tariffs, and for
a time even her own defence forces. The Finns were citizens of
Finland as well as subjects of the Tsar. Their leaders thus were in a
position to negotiate with the Russian Government almost like
representatives of a foreign power. For the Finns, relations with
Russia was foreign policy. And for the Russian Government relations

3

with Finland could never be reduced to being solely a domestic matter of the Russian empire, even though from the end of the nineteenth century Russian policy aimed at this by trying to do away with Finnish self-government. The Finnish question always remained to some degree part of Russian foreign policy; it was affected by the actions of other powers and by events elsewhere in the world.

Above all it was of course affected by the actions of the Finns themselves. The fact that Finland did exercise some choice in her foreign policy at that time is brought out by the intensity of the debate among Finns on how to deal with Russia: between the conservatives who advocated appeasement of Russian power and prestige as the safest means of preserving the essentials of Finnish national life; the liberals who insisted on standing fast on constitutional rights to the point of offering passive resistance to Russian violations of the Finnish autonomy; the activists who prepared for direct action by sending young men to Germany for military training; and the left-wing revolutionaries who made common cause with their Russian friends in the belief that the overthrow of the Tsarist regime would bring both liberation and social transformation.[2]

The declaration of Finnish independence in 1917 did not put an end to the controversy and the struggle between the different parties, though it transposed them to a new plane. The attainment of sovereignty of course removed the legal and other formal obstacles that had hampered the pursuit of Finland's national interests in relation to other nations. But it did not by itself solve either the internal or the external problems facing Finland, nor did it settle her place in the world. 6th December 1917 was neither an end nor a beginning: it was a high point in a continuing process.

The course in foreign policy chosen by the first Government of independent Finland was set by the facts of power prevailing in Northern and Eastern Europe at the time, by the Finnish experience of the preceding century, and not least by internal conditions.

Although Lenin's Government had been the first to recognize the independence of Finland on the last day of 1917, Russia remained in Finnish eyes the natural enemy of the country's freedom. The change of regime that had taken place in Petrograd did not erase memories of Tsarist oppression. The Bolsheviks were suspected of relying on subversion to bring back to the Soviet Union what had been lost by Russia; forty thousand Russian troops had remained in Finland even after the declaration of independence, and the Finnish

4

working class was in a revolutionary ferment. To the conservatives then in power in Finland, the only solid bulwark against the spread of Communism and chaos seemed to be the Kaiser's Germany, whose armies at the end of 1917, and indeed far into 1918, were undisputed masters of Eastern Europe. Finland's foreign policy therefore was anchored to German support. Germany, it was hoped, would take care of Finnish interests at the peace settlement that was expected to end the world war. Germany was to see to it that Finland would expand beyond her historical frontiers into Eastern Karelia. The election of a German prince as King of Finland was to ensure that Germany would continue to protect Finnish independence. German troops were invited to come to Finland in the spring of 1918 to help defeat the Reds in the civil war that had broken out in January of that year, and German experts were brought in to organize the Finnish Army.

This policy collapsed with the capitulation of Germany in November 1918. By that time Finland had become compromised in Western eyes, and a complete about-turn in Finnish policy was necessary. The German King-elect abdicated in December 1918 before setting foot on Finnish soil. The pro-German political leaders stood aside. In the first parliamentary elections at the beginning of 1919 the republicans gained a large majority. Only then, in May 1919, did the United States and Britain agree to recognize Finland, and France confirm her recognition which had been withdrawn in the previous year.[3]

Relations with Russia remained unsettled. In 1919 the White Russians tried to induce the Finns to join their abortive attack against the Russian capital, and the idea of leading an anti-Bolshevik crusade did tempt General C. G. Mannerheim, the former Tsarist officer who had returned to his native Finland after the Revolution to lead the Whites to victory in the civil war. Minor excursions into Eastern Karelia were made by Finnish irregular formations. But intervention in the Russian civil war received no substantial support, especially as the White Russians strenuously opposed Allied recognition of Finnish independence; and in the first presidential election in 1919 Mannerheim was defeated by K. J. Ståhlberg, the liberal candidate.[4]

Yet a state of war was considered to exist between Finland and Russia, on the ground that Russian troops had joined the Finnish Reds in the civil war, and a formal peace conference was held in the latter half of 1920 in Tartu (Estonia). The question of Eastern

Karelia caused the greatest difficulties. The area, though it had never been part of Finland, had a Finnish-speaking population. Finland demanded that the people of Eastern Karelia be given the right freely to determine their allegiance. The Soviet Government refused to agree, and in the end the Finns had to be content with a unilateral Soviet declaration promising Eastern Karelia autonomy within the Soviet Union. In the Tartu Treaty, which was signed in October 1920, the Soviet Government reaffirmed its recognition of an independent Finland within the borders of the former Grand Duchy, with the addition of the Petsamo area giving Finland access to the Arctic and valuable nickel deposits.[5] If this result failed to satisfy nationalist opinion in Finland, it was equally unsatisfactory to the Soviet Government which had asked for additional ground on the Karelian Isthmus to provide depth to the defence of Leningrad, or alternatively for some islands in the Gulf of Finland along the approaches to the city. In 1920 the Soviet Union was too weak to enforce such claims, but they were not forgotten: less than twenty years later the borders drawn at Tartu were taken up for revision.

While claiming for the East Karelians the right to self-determination, the Finnish Government was wholly opposed to giving it to the people of the Aaland islands. The islanders, whose language is Swedish, wished to attach themselves to Sweden, and the Swedish Government actively supported their separatist movement. But in 1921 the League of Nations, to which the dispute was submitted, preferred the Finnish contention that geographically and historically the islands had always been part of Finland. At the same time, the Aaland islands were demilitarized and neutralized, and the convention to that effect was signed in October 1921 by ten nations, including the Great Powers and all the states bordering on the Baltic Sea – except for the Soviet Union which at the time was not a member of the League. Later efforts to induce the Soviet Union to join the convention failed, though not because of any lack of Soviet interest in the fate of the Aaland islands.[6]

The recognition of the Great Powers, the Treaty of Tartu, the settlement of the Aaland dispute, and, finally, membership in the League of Nations, established the identity of Finland among the independent states of Europe. Having cut off her early bonds with Germany, Finland was free of foreign political commitments. This had its obvious advantages; it also bred a feeling of lonely insecurity. Yet an attempt in 1922 to draw Finland into security arrangements between Russia's western neighbours failed to get support in Parliament; a substantial majority was reluctant to let the country be involved with nations with whom Finland had little in common. This reaction contained the seed of a policy of neutrality. But there were attitudes in Finland that were far from neutral. Nationalist opinion continued to clamour for the liberation of the Finnish-speaking people of Eastern Karelia and entertained dreams of a Greater Finland including all the Finnish tribes lost in the vast sea of Soviet peoples. In a search for relatives the linguistic bonds with the Estonians and Hungarians were actively cultivated, while the feud between the two language groups within the country, the Finnish-speaking majority and the Swedish-speaking minority, disturbed relations with Sweden and the other Scandinavian nations. Finland in the 1920s was undecided, as it were, whether she belonged to Scandinavia or the Baltic states. Her foreign policy in this period is hard to define. Indeed, there was no foreign policy to define: the League of Nations was supposed to look after the security of its members.

It was not until the 1930s, when faith in the League had turned to disillusion, that the search for security became the leading theme of Finnish foreign policy. A non-aggression treaty with the Soviet Union in 1932 was the first step towards a policy of neutrality. Hitler's advance foreshadowed a reign of force and violence in Europe: the problem for Finland, as for most small nations, was how to avoid being drawn into a conflict between the Great Powers. Then, in December 1935, the Finnish Parliament unanimously approved a Government resolution declaring Finland's adherence to Scandinavian neutrality. The neutrality of Finland, it was stated, could best be preserved in association with the other Scandinavian nations whose loyalty to the concept of neutrality was universally acknowledged.[7]

The same could not be said at the time of Finland's own neutrality. The Social-Democratic Governments of the other Scandinavian states regarded their eastern partner with a great deal of reserve. In their eyes, the Finland of President P. E. Svinhufvud (1931–37) was a seat of reaction. The Soviet attitude was of course all the more suspicious. Svinhufvud had been Regent in the pro-German period of 1917–18; when he was Prime Minister, in 1930, the Finnish Communist Party had been declared illegal and membership of it treason; as President he refused to admit even the Social-Democrats into the Government. The Finnish attitude to the Soviet Union, especially in opinion-making circles, was one of intense hostility. The East Karelian issue continued to engage the emotions of nationalist youth. Trade with the Soviet Union was negligible, cultural relations practically non-existent. It was a time of Finnish MacCarthyism.

The change of regime that took place in Finland in 1937 opened a new era in foreign relations. Svinhufvud was defeated by Kyösti Kallio, leader of the middle-of-the-road Agrarian Party, in the presidential election, and the Government was taken over by a new coalition which for the first time since the civil war of 1918 included the Social-Democrats as partners with the Agrarians and the Liberals. This brought Finland ideologically into line with the other Scandinavian states. In Moscow, the change was hailed as a victory of the 'peace-loving forces' in their struggle against fascist aggression. The new Finnish Government did indeed demonstratively cold-shoulder Germany. Foreign Minister Rudolf Holsti's first visit abroad, in February 1937, was to Moscow. His purpose was to dispel suspicions of Finnish-German collusion and assure the Soviet leaders that Finland wished to preserve her neutrality. He may have succeeded better than had been intended, for in April 1938 the Soviet Foreign Minister told the American Ambassador that as a result of the German annexation of Austria countries like Finland seemed to be disposed to look for Soviet support for their independence against possible German aggression. And in that same month the Soviet Government secretly approached the Finnish Government with an offer of military assistance in the event of a German attempt to use Finland as a base of aggression against the Soviet Union.

This was far more than Holsti had bargained for. The Finnish Government had no wish to substitute Soviet for German protection: it hoped to persuade both to strike out Finland from their strategic calculations. This it believed could best be achieved through close identification with the other Scandinavian states. From time to time there was even talk of a Scandinavian defence alliance, but this was a stillborn idea. The Scandinavian nations could not agree on a common enemy: the Finns feared Russia and the Danes feared Germany; the Swedes could not make up their minds which they ought to fear; the Norwegians believed themselves to be safe from both. A more realistic concept was that put forward by Sweden's Foreign minister Rickard Sandler: military co-operation between two or more Scandinavian nations in limited areas and with limited commitments. The Aaland islands were an obvious point for such co-operation. In the hands of a Great Power, as Napoleon had once put it, Aaland would have been a 'pistol aimed at the heart of Sweden'; with this in mind Swedish military planners were anxious to fill the vacuum created by the Aaland Convention of 1921. In the course of 1938 a joint Finnish-Swedish plan for the defence of the islands was worked out; in January 1939 it was formally confirmed by the two Governments. Since a revision of the Convention was necessary, the plan was to be submitted to the other signatory powers as well as to the League of Nations for approval. Significantly, the Swedish Government insisted that Soviet consent also be obtained. In the Swedish view, the potential threat to the Aaland islands came from Germany. Besides, Swedish opinion was not prepared to accept a commitment that might involve Sweden in a Finnish-Soviet conflict.

The Finnish Government, therefore, in August 1938, responded to the Soviet offer of support by proposing that the Soviet Government agree to the projected measures for the defence of Aaland in return for an undertaking by Finland not to allow any foreign power to use Finland as a base of aggression against the Soviet Union. This failed to satisfy the Russians. Without Soviet help, they argued, Finland would be incapable of protecting her neutrality; the Germans were bound to force their way in; and the Red Army was not prepared to remain on the border to wait for the enemy but would advance as far as possible to meet him. Only a Finnish promise to accept military assistance from the Soviet Union could be regarded as a sufficient guarantee for Soviet security. As for the Aaland islands, the Soviet Government had no objection to their remilitarization provided the Soviet Union, instead of Sweden, could take part in the project. In addition the Soviet Government claimed the right to establish a base on the Finnish island of Hogland in the Gulf of Finland; this, it said, was necessary for the defence of Leningrad.

The Soviet proposals were rejected by the Finnish Government on the grounds that their acceptance would violate Finnish sovereignty and conflict with the policy of neutrality pursued by Finland together with the Scandinavian states. In later contacts between the two governments, in December 1938 and March 1939, the Soviet demands were limited to the use of Hogland and three smaller islands in the Gulf, but the Finnish Government refused to make any territorial concessions. As a result the Finnish-Swedish plan to remilitarize the Aaland islands ran into Soviet opposition at the

League of Nations in May 1939. The Soviet Government claimed it had at least as much right as Sweden to act as guardian of the islands. This had an immediate effect on the Swedish Government: the bill requesting Parliament to authorize the implementation of the Aaland plan was withdrawn.

For Finland the collapse of the Aaland plan meant a double defeat. It exposed Swedish unwillingness to support Finland at the risk of a conflict with the Soviet Union. It also revealed the failure of the efforts to gain Soviet confidence in Finnish neutrality. Verbal assurances of neutrality were not enough. This was clearly brought out by the Anglo-French-Soviet negotiations in the spring and summer of 1939. The Soviet Government insisted that a three-power guarantee against German aggression, direct or indirect, be given to Finland and the other border states, regardless of whether these states wanted it – and none of them wished to be so protected. Though the talks ended in failure, the Western Powers did in effect accept the contention that the Soviet Union was entitled, in the name of its own security, to take action to prevent its neighbours from falling under German influence. The Soviet Union, too, had its Monroe Doctrine and Finland was part of the area it covered.

Finnish policy in the late 'thirties had been based on the unspoken assumption of permanent hostility between Germany and the Soviet Union; this would maintain the balance of power in the Baltic area. The assumption was shattered in August 1939. The secret protocol attached to the Soviet-German pact of non-aggression was of course not known at the time; but what the Soviet Government had asked for in its talks with Britain and France was known; it was easy to guess that it must have obtained from Hitler what it had failed to extract from the Western Powers. The consequences of the pact for the border states soon became apparent. In the space of two weeks counting from Ribbentrop's second visit to Moscow in late September 1939, the Soviet Government imposed upon the three Baltic states, Estonia, Latvia and Lithuania, mutual assistance treaties which gave Soviet forces access to all the military bases south of the Gulf of Finland that they had lost in the First World War. And on 5th October the Finnish Government was invited to send a delegation to Moscow.

The man chosen to negotiate on behalf of Finland was J. K. Paasikivi, a former leader of the Conservative Party who at the time was Finnish Minister to Stockholm. He had headed the Finnish delegation at the Tartu conference in 1920, and although impeccably conservative in his outlook and therefore above suspicion of any 'softness toward Communism', he had always belonged to the school of thought that had advocated a policy of conciliation with Russia, recognition of her strategic interests, and avoidance of provocative attitudes that might challenge Russian prestige. At a later stage in the negotiations he was joined by the then Minister of Finance, Väinö Tanner, who was the leader of the Social-Democratic Party.

Paasikivi's instructions made it clear that Finland, unlike the Baltic states, would not compromise her independence or her neutrality. This resolution was backed up by military preparations: on 11th October, the day Paasikivi arrived in Moscow, the Government called up all reserve contingents for 'refresher courses', which amounted to disguised mobilization.

On the Soviet side, Stalin himself conducted the negotiations. His demands, and the reasoning behind them, closely followed the traditional lines of Russian strategic thinking. Whoever emerged as victor in the World War, he argued, would inevitably attack the Soviet Union. The pact with Germany was no eternal guarantee: 'Everything in this world can change'. The aggressor was bound to use Finnish territory in order to get at Leningrad, and Finland would be powerless to stop him. For this reason the Finnish-Soviet border on the Karelian Isthmus had to be pushed farther north so as to remove Leningrad from within the range of modern artillery on the Finnish side. Finland also had to cede the islands in the Gulf of Finland, as well as the western part of the Fisherman's Peninsula near Petsamo on the Arctic. Further, Finland was to lease to the Soviet Union the Peninsula of Hanko on the southern coast of Finland west of Helsinki: the purpose was to establish there a Soviet naval base with coastal artillery; this, according to Stalin, was necessary to enable the Soviet Union to close the entrance to the Gulf of Finland. In exchange, Finland was to get an area in Eastern Karelia twice as large as the combined areas of the territories to be ceded and would be allowed to fortify the Aaland islands provided no other power took part in the project. Stalin also agreed to abandon his initial demand for a mutual assistance treaty.

Stalin's plan for the security of Leningrad seemed to be based on the defence system of the Tsars. Finnish military experts argued that this was out of date; the security of Leningrad, in their view, was entirely dependent on who held the southern shores of the Gulf of

Finland. But such arguments were brushed aside by Stalin with the reminder that in 1919 the White Russians under Yudenitch had attacked along the Gulf and later the British had done the same. He insisted from the beginning that his demands had not been put forward for bargaining purposes but represented Russia's minimum security requirements. The Finnish Government now retreated from its previous stand on the indivisibility of Finnish territory. It was prepared to yield ground on the Karelian Isthmus, though not so much as Stalin had asked for, and give up some of the islands in the Gulf. But it refused to lease Hanko. Stalin then agreed to shift the site of the Soviet base to some islands off the Hanko Peninsula, but this made no difference. Finnish opinion was not convinced of Stalin's defensive purpose. A Soviet base close to the Finnish capital was regarded as an intolerable threat, not only to the neutrality but to the very independence of Finland. On this issue the talks broke down, and on 13th November the Finnish delegates left Moscow.

In the meantime the Finnish Government was making extensive efforts to secure foreign support. The results were meagre. Germany, faithful to its pact with the Soviet Union, advised the Finns to be sensible and give in. Britain gave them no encouragement; as Winston Churchill pointed out at the time, the bases sought by the Soviet Union could be used only against Germany. President Roosevelt's offers of mediation were contemptuously dismissed by Molotov. The Scandinavian nations did display their sympathy for Finland at a meeting of all four Heads of State in Stockholm; but behind the scenes the Swedish Government once again refused to implement the Aaland plan. The Finnish Government knew that it stood alone. This did not deter it. No one seriously believed that Stalin might go to war. Some of the reserves were even allowed to return home after the breakdown of the Moscow talks. Finland prepared herself for a prolonged period of pressure and tension.

The phoney peace was soon shattered. On 26th November the Soviet Government claimed that Finnish artillery had fired on Soviet troops on the Karelian Isthmus and demanded the withdrawal of Finnish troops to a distance of 20–25 kilometres from the border. When the Finnish Government refused to do so unilaterally, the Soviet Government on 28th November cancelled the non-aggression treaty of 1932. On 30th November Helsinki was bombed by Soviet aircraft and Soviet troops crossed the border in force. And on the same day Moscow revealed that it had set up a 'democratic government of Finland' composed of Finnish Communists in exile. It was headed by O. V. Kuusinen, a former leader of the Reds in the Finnish civil war, who had fled to Russia in 1918 and since then risen to a prominent position in the Comintern.

If the Soviet leaders believed that Kuusinen's government would rally the Finnish workers to the side of the invaders, they had utterly misread the mood of the Finnish people. The civil war could no longer be rekindled. Whatever internal differences and doubts had existed were wiped out by the open challenge to Finnish sovereignty which the Kuusinen government embodied. The question of whether fresh concessions ought to have been offered to avoid war became irrelevant: the Soviet Union only recognized the Kuusinen government and rejected all attempts to resume negotiations. The choice was one between war and unconditional surrender.

The Finnish forces, though heavily outnumbered, succeeded in stopping the Soviet advance on the Karelian Isthmus. Along the eastern border large columns of invaders were annihilated. By Christmas the entire Soviet offensive had bogged down. This achievement amazed the world and probably not least the Soviet leaders who apparently had expected an easy march into Helsinki. At the beginning of January 1940 Marshal Voroshilov himself took over command of the Finnish campaign; a complete reorganization of the Soviet forces was undertaken; reinforcements were brought in. But in the meantime Finland had a breathing space, and her Government made every effort to obtain outside aid.

In spite of world-wide sympathy and admiration for Finland's fight, this proved to be a frustrating task. The League of Nations rose from its deathbed to expel the Soviet Union from membership, but this had no visible effect on Moscow. Germany was neutral to the point of denying transit for arms deliveries to Finland. In Sweden, Sandler, the Foreign Minister who had actively worked for co-operation with Finland, had been forced to resign, and the new Government formed in December virtually ruled out military intervention in the Finnish war. In the United States, Finland's efforts to obtain arms and credits were obstructed by the neutrality laws which prevented the Administration from taking sides in a European war. In Britain and France, too, the Governments were at first reluctant to get involved in a struggle that seemed doomed to fail. But the initial success of Finland's defence changed their minds. The Allied Governments were under pressure from public opinion to do something to save Finland. A northern expedition also appeared to offer a chance to hit at Germany from a new direction. On their way to Finland the Allied forces could take over control of the Norwegian coast and occupy Sweden's iron ore mines. On 5th February 1940 the Supreme War Council decided to send an expeditionary corps to Scandinavia, provided Finland appealed for such aid. The refusal of the Swedish and Norwegian Governments to let the Allies through was not taken seriously; as a last resort Allied troops were to force their way in.

The Allied plan of intervention may well have induced the Soviet Government to reconsider its Finnish policy. Stalin's declared purpose was to keep the Soviet Union out of the war between Germany and the West. The Finnish campaign, if it were to drag on, threatened to involve Soviet forces in a clash with the Allies. At the beginning of February the Soviet Government let it be known through Stockholm that it was prepared to resume negotiations with the Finnish Government. Kuusinen was no longer mentioned. For the Finns, this in itself was a momentous victory. But Russian prestige was now in need of repair: the peace terms were far in excess of Stalin's original demands. In addition to Hanko and the islands, Finland was asked to cede the entire Province of Viipuri. To back up this demand Soviet forces in February began a new offensive on the Karelian Isthmus, far more powerful and more skilfully led than in December; the Finnish defence line on the road to Viipuri was soon broken.

Throughout February and in the first week of March the Finnish Government was torn between the uncertainties of Allied aid and the awful prospect of peace on Soviet terms. The choice before it had a significance far beyond Finland's own fate. Acceptance of Allied aid could have plunged all Scandinavia into war; it might have unhinged the power alignments of the Second World War. But in view of the refusal of Sweden and Norway to grant transit it seemed uncertain whether the Allied troops could ever reach Finland; in any event most of them were intended for Norway and Sweden; the small contingents destined for the Finnish front were likely to be too few and too late. On 7th March 1940 a delegation headed by Risto Ryti, the Prime Minister, travelled to Moscow; on 12th March, the last deadline set by the Allies for a Finnish appeal for aid, a peace treaty was signed; on the following day fighting came to an end.

Finland ceded the entire Province of Viipuri up to the frontier of Peter the Great–a far larger area than the one that the Finnish forces had had to yield in the course of the fighting. The islands in the Gulf of Finland were also ceded as well as parts of the districts of Salla and Kuusamo in the north-eastern part of the country; in addition Finland was required to build a railway from the new border at Salla up to Kemijärvi where it could be linked with the line leading to the Swedish frontier. Finland further had to lease the Hanko area to the Soviet Union for use as a naval base.

The Peace Treaty of Moscow expressed in its preamble the conviction of the two Governments that 'the creation of precise conditions of reciprocal security' corresponded to the interests of both parties. In reality, the Treaty turned out to be merely an agreement to stop the fighting rather than a basis for stable and peaceful relations between the two countries. On the Finnish side, at any rate, it created an acute sense of insecurity. After the Winter War, opinion in Finland was even less inclined to trust Soviet intentions than in 1939. Finnish suspicions were further sharpened by the course of Soviet policy in 1940. The Soviet Government effectively opposed attempts made during 1940 to form a Finnish-Swedish alliance or union, alleging that this project was directed against the Soviet Union. The Soviet Government also demanded the demilitarization of the Aaland islands. It asked for a share in the exploitation of the Petsamo nickel mines. It claimed a right of way by rail to the Hanko base. It put pressure on the Finnish Government to remove Tanner, the Social-Democratic leader, from his post as Minister of Supply. It lent diplomatic support to the activities of left-wing groups in Finland. It warned the Finns not to elect as President any one of four possible candidates distrusted by Moscow.

In retrospect, all these Soviet actions can be fitted into the pattern of the defensive policy pursued by the Soviet Union with great single-mindedness ever since the late 'thirties. When Stalin had told Paasikivi in October 1939 that he was only asking for the minimum required by Soviet security, he had probably meant precisely what he had said. The German victories in the West made him look for maximum security. As an immediate reaction to the fall of France the Soviet Union annexed the three Baltic states. But Finland remained free, and Finnish opinion was embittered by the losses of the Winter War. The Soviet leaders seem to have been obsessed with the danger of her joining Germany. But if the purpose of their policy was to prevent this from happening, its effect was only to strengthen the tendencies it was supposed to suppress. It created in Finland the impression that the Soviet Union was carrying on its attack of the previous winter by political means with the aim of taking over Finland as it had taken over the Baltic states. No effective assistance could be expected from Sweden and none from the West; after the German occupation of Denmark and Norway, Petsamo on the Arctic was Finland's only remaining opening to the West.

In this situation the Finnish leaders responded with relief to the first hint of support from Germany. This came in August 1940, when Hitler had begun preparations for his eastern campaign. Finland was offered the chance of buying arms from Germany in return for allowing German troops to pass through Finland to Norway. Sweden had already agreed to a similar German request, while Finland had just granted the Soviet Union right of transit to the Hanko base. In these circumstances the Finnish leaders regarded their transit agreement with Germany as a useful counterweight to Soviet pressure rather than as a dangerous commitment. In fact, however, it proved to be the point of no return for Finnish policy. It was the first step in a systematic German campaign to tie Finland to Hitler's war plans. Actually relatively few German troops were moved through Finland: by May 1941 altogether only 14,000 men had used the Finnish route, while more than a quarter of a million were transported through Sweden in 1940 alone. The transit agreement with Finland was in reality a cover for the future movement of German troops from Norway, not back to Germany, but into the Soviet Union.[8]

The appearance of German troops on Finnish soil was a clear breach of the German-Soviet agreement of 1939, and Molotov did not fail to point this out in his talks with Hitler in Berlin in November 1940. He asked the Germans to keep their hands off Finland; the Soviet Government, he explained, intended to solve the Finnish question in the manner it had applied to Bessarabia and the Baltic states. Hitler refused, however, to withdraw the German troops from Finland and warned Molotov that Germany was opposed to a new conflict in the Baltic area. Disagreement on Finland was one of the principal reasons for the failure of the Berlin talks.

Soon after Molotov had left Berlin Hitler confirmed the plans for a grand offensive against Russia. Finland was assigned an active role in it but the Finns themselves had no knowledge of this at the time. Elaborate precautions were taken by the Germans to conceal their intentions. In the spring of 1941 informal talks were held between Finnish and German military authorities, but the subject of these was co-operation in the event of a Soviet attack, and no binding agreements were made. In May the Germans went so far as to ask the Finnish Government to submit points to be taken up in imaginary negotiations with Moscow, and at the same time a high German official was sent to Helsinki to assure President Risto Ryti that there would be no war before 1942. But in the second week of June German troops ostensibly in transit from Norway to Germany began massing in Finnish Lapland. On 14th June the Finnish Government was informed that war with Russia was imminent. Three days later the Finnish Army was mobilized. Finnish troops in Lapland were put under German command, and on 22nd June, the day the German invasion was set in motion, Hitler announced that in the north his troops stood 'side by side' with their Finnish comrades.

Formally, the Finnish Government was still uncommitted, and its first reaction to Hitler's announcement was to declare its neutrality. But the mood in Finland was not neutral. The German invasion of Russia was seen to provide release from the continued Soviet threat as well as an opportunity to recover what had been lost in 1940. In any case, with the German troops in Lapland poised for attack and Soviet forces in their base in Hanko, neutrality could hardly have been maintained for long. In fact it lasted four days, for on 25th June the Soviet Union launched air attacks on Finnish territory, and in the evening of that day the Government declared that Finland was at war with the Soviet Union. Parliament unanimously passed a vote of confidence.

In June the Finnish forces had taken up defensive positions along the Soviet border. At the end of the month they regrouped for offensive action. On 10th July they began their advance. In two months they recaptured the territory that had been ceded in 1940. But the advance was carried on into Soviet Karelia and was not halted until it had reached, in December 1941, the Syväri (Soir) river connecting Lake Onega with Lake Ladoga.

In the official Finnish view, Finland was waging a separate war, coinciding with but not part of the German-Soviet struggle. It was called the 'Continuation War' – the Second Round of the conflict that had opened in November 1939. Finland was not an ally of Germany:

she was a co-belligerent. She was not a German satellite: Nazi ideology made little headway in Finland and attempts to impose it were firmly rejected. She fought for her own ends, not those of Germany: German requests for Finnish participation in the offensive against Leningrad or the Murmansk Railway were refused. The occupation of Soviet Karelia was justified by the Finnish Government on military grounds, as a measure designed to create depth for the defence of Finland, without commitment in regard to the political future of the area.

The Finnish case at first met with some sympathy in the West. But soon it came under fire from both sides. As a result of German pressure Finland took the initiative in breaking diplomatic relations with Britain in August 1941. The United States and Britain for their part made several attempts during 1941 to persuade Finland to make peace or at least stop fighting. The Finnish Government rejected these advances partly because it probably still believed in a German victory, and partly because it had no faith in the ability of the Western Powers to protect Finnish interests at a future settlement. As a result Britain declared war on Finland in December 1941. The United States refrained from doing so and continued its efforts to extricate Finland from the war.

After the German defeat at Stalingrad the Finnish Government became actively interested in disengaging itself. Its freedom of action was limited, however, by Finland's dependence on Germany for food and other essential imports, as well as by fear of German retaliation. When at the beginning of 1943 the Finnish Government asked Sweden and the United States to mediate between Finland and the Soviet Union,[9] Berlin threatened to take 'extreme action' and stopped food deliveries. This deterred the Finns from pursuing their enquiries for a time. But at the end of the year they did make contact with the Soviet Government through Sweden, and at the beginning of 1944 two delegates were sent to Moscow to find out at what price peace might be had. The demands they brought back were that the Finnish forces had to withdraw behind the 1940 borders, Petsamo was to be ceded in exchange for Hanko, and the German troops were to be interned or expelled within a month; in addition Finland was to pay an indemnity of 600 million dollars. Both the expulsion of the Germans and the indemnity were judged to exceed Finnish capacities, while giving up all the territory regained seemed unreasonable at a time when Finnish troops still stood along the Syväri river.

The Government wanted peace but still hoped to get it at a cheaper price. The Soviet terms were rejected. This did not save the country from German retaliation. Hitler let it be known that no arms could be sold to Finland so long as there was no guarantee of her not defecting, and a little later grain deliveries from Germany were again stopped.

On the Soviet side the refusal of the peace terms was followed by a steady build-up of Soviet forces on the Finnish front. On 9th June 1944, as the Allies were landing in Normandy, more than twenty Soviet infantry divisions, under the cover of one of the most devastating artillery barrages of the Second World War and backed by more than 400 bomber planes, launched an offensive against the Finnish lines on the narrow front of the Karelian Isthmus. They broke through on the west coast along the road to Viipuri; the Finnish forces had to withdraw all along the Isthmus, and from Soviet Karelia as well, to avoid encirclement. On 22nd June the Finnish Government asked for peace through Stockholm, but the reply received on the following day was that Moscow now insisted on unconditional surrender. On that same day von Ribbentrop, the German Foreign Minister, arrived in Helsinki unannounced to offer military assistance on condition that Finland commit herself not to make a separate peace. The Finnish Government thus faced the agonizing choice of surrender or a fight to the bitter end. The dilemma was resolved by President Ryti who gave the pledge required by Ribbentrop in the form of a personal letter to Hitler. He thus deliberately exceeded his constitutional powers so as to avoid committing the Finnish Government. His personal word was enough for the Germans who sent both troops and arms to the Karelian Isthmus. The German troops had little significance, but the modern weapons received from Germany were important. By the middle of July the Soviet offensive was stopped before it had reached the 1940 border.

The time gained by Finland proved to have decisive value. On 1st August, Ryti resigned, and his successor, Marshal Mannerheim, informed the Germans that he did not regard Ryti's pledge as binding. The Soviet divisions on the Finnish front were urgently required for the race to Berlin: the Soviet Government no longer insisted on unconditional surrender. At the end of August the Finnish Government received word through Stockholm that the Soviet Government was prepared to enter into peace negotiations provided Finland broke off relations with Germany and demanded the evacuation of German troops from Finnish territory. This condition having been fulfilled on 2nd September, a ceasefire came into force on 4th-5th September; on 6th September a Finnish delegation left for Moscow; an Armistice Agreement was signed on 19th September.

The Armistice Agreement reconfirmed the terms of the Peace Treaty of 1940, with a number of changes and additions. The most important of these were: Petsamo was to be ceded; instead of Hanko, the Porkkala Peninsula close to the Finnish capital was to be leased for fifty years for use as a naval base; Finland had to pay a war indemnity of 300 million pre-war dollars in the form of goods to be delivered in six years; all 'fascist' organizations had to be banned; German property and assets were to be frozen (later to be handed over to the Soviet Union); persons accused of war crimes were to be arrested and tried; the Finnish merchant fleet was to be placed at the disposal of the Allied Powers; an Allied Control Commission was to be installed in Helsinki.

The armistice with the Soviet Union was not the end of the war for Finland. The German troops in the north, a force of 200,000 men, did not leave Finland voluntarily, and it took another military campaign to force them into Norway. In the course of their withdrawal the Germans laid waste the entire Province of Lapland: this was Hitler's revenge for Finland's treachery, as he called it, in making peace before Germany's final doom.

Finland emerged from the war a crippled nation. The number of killed had been close to 90,000, out of a population of little more than four million. The cession of territory, more than one-tenth of Finland's total area, severely reduced her industrial capacity. The economy was exhausted by years of war, during which as much as 16 per cent of the nation had been in uniform. Foreign trade was at a standstill, the merchant fleet in Allied hands. Houses and work and farms had to be found for the 400,000 people of the ceded areas, all of whom had chosen to leave their homes and move west of the new border. Industry had to be expanded at a forced pace to produce the goods required by the Soviet Union as war reparations.

The political structure underwent an equally drastic change. The Communist Party was legalized and its members emerged from prison or underground bent upon carrying out a complete break with the past. In the first post-war elections in the spring of 1945 the Communists and the left-wing Socialists allied with them took a quarter of the seats in Parliament. The Government which then came into power followed the pattern that at the time prevailed in many European countries: it was a coalition of the Agrarian Party, the Social-Democrats and the Communists.

Superficially the situation in Finland appeared to be similar to that in the other western neighbours of the Soviet Union. There was, however, one vital distinction. Finland, though defeated, had not been conquered. Apart from Britain and the Soviet Union, Finland was the only one of the European nations involved in the Second World War to avert a military occupation. The continuity of her political institutions was unbroken; her social fabric was intact. The outcome of the war thus in effect confirmed Finland's continued existence as an independent state and a Western democracy. The Finns still had control over their own affairs, although to retain it they had to bend themselves, as they had done in 1918, to the prevailing facts of power.

III. *The Peace of Paris*

ON 14TH AUGUST 1946 THE FINNISH GOVERNMENT RECEIVED
an invitation from the Conference of twenty-one Allied and Asso-
ciated Powers which had convened in Paris at the end of July to
make peace with their lesser enemies in the Second World War.
Finland, along with Italy, Bulgaria, Hungary and Rumania, was
asked to send a delegation to present its views on the terms of peace.
The Finnish Government had anticipated the invitation. A strong
Finnish delegation had arrived in Paris a day before the invitation
was issued. It was headed by the Prime Minister, Mr Mauno Pekkala, and included three other members of the Cabinet as well as
leading representatives of Parliament. It was accompanied by Finland's foremost experts on international law, defence, finance and
industry. It carried with it detailed instructions issued by the president of the Republic, Juho Kusti Paasikivi, and approved by the
Foreign Affairs Committee of Parliament.

The Finns thus had come to Paris willing and able to negotiate on
all aspects and every detail of the proposed treaty of peace. They
were met, not with hostility, but with amiable indifference. The
victorious powers were not interested in negotiating with their former enemies. That was not what the Paris Conference was for. This
was made clear at the outset. One of the first decisions of the Conference was that representatives of former enemy states, though they
would be granted a hearing, must not be permitted to attend meetings except when specifically invited to do so. This rule was enforced
rigorously. At the first meeting of the Commission dealing with the
political and territorial clauses of the treaty with Finland, Prime
Minister Pekkala together with some of his colleagues came to listen
from the press gallery. But as soon as they were spotted they were
asked to leave: former enemies were to be heard not seen. Yet it was
an open meeting, and the journalists, including those from Finland,

C. G. E. Mannerheim, Marshal of Finland,
President from 1944–46.

*President Kyösti Kallio visited Stockholm in 1938
where he was received by King Gustav V.*

*Minister J. K. Paasikivi on his way to the Moscow
negotiations on October 9, 1939. At the railway
station in Helsinki he was seen off by Prime Minister
A. K. Cajander and the Speaker of Parliament,
Väinö Hakkila.*

were allowed to stay. From then on the press provided virtually the sole link between the Finnish delegation and the Conference.

Finland did have her day in court: the Foreign Minister, Mr Carl Enckell, on 15th August 1946, put the Finnish case at a plenary meeting. A little later, Finland's Commander-in-Chief, General Sihvo, was invited to attend a meeting of the Military Commission, but as he had nothing to add to the Finnish views presented in writing and no member of the Commission could think of anything to ask him, his appearance lasted only a couple of minutes. That was the only occasion on which the Conference considered it necessary to consult the Finnish delegation. After waiting for a couple of weeks the Finnish experts began to drift away. Prime Minister Pekkala and most of his colleagues found they would be more usefully employed at home. Only Foreign Minister Enckell with a few officials of his Ministry stayed on till the end.

It was not Enckell's first peace conference. He had been in Paris in 1919 arguing the Finnish case on the Aaland island issue with the victors of the First World War. At that time the map of Europe had been drawn and redrawn in endless sessions and petitioners had had a free run of the conference. Paris in 1946 was different. The Allies of the Second World War were determined to avoid repetition of the untidy ways of peace-making employed after the First World War. The boundaries of Europe had been drawn by the victorious armies; they were not to be redrawn by the diplomats in Paris.

The Big Three had decided at Potsdam that the peace treaties with Italy, Rumania, Bulgaria, Hungary and Finland were to be drawn up by the Council of Foreign Ministers representing the 'five principal powers' (the United States, the U.S.S.R., Britain, France and China). It had also been decided that not all the five powers would be parties to the drafting of each of the five treaties. For each of the treaties, the Council would be composed of the members representing those states which were signatory to the terms of surrender or armistice imposed upon the enemy state concerned. For the purpose of the peace settlement for Italy, France was to be regarded as a signatory to the terms of surrender for Italy. At the first meeting of the Council in London in October 1945, the Americans and Russians failed to agree on how to interpret this decision. Secretary of State James Byrnes thought it meant that all members of the Council could take part in discussing all the treaties, though only those who had signed the surrender or armistice agreement were entitled to vote. Foreign Minister Molotov insisted that those who had not signed the surrender or armistice agreement could not even be present when the peace treaty was discussed. The Soviet interpretation meant the exclusion of the United States from the consideration of the Finnish treaty and of France from the consideration of all but one treaty, while China was to be excluded altogether. As a compromise Byrnes finally agreed to the Soviet view on condition that a larger peace conference be convened to give not only all the principal powers but smaller allies as well the opportunity to state their views on all the treaties. This proposal was accepted by Molotov at the meeting of the Foreign Ministers of the United States, the Soviet Union and Britain in Moscow in December 1945. It was agreed at the same time, however, that the larger peace conference could only make recommendations on the drafts prepared by the Council of Foreign Ministers which would retain the power to decide on the final texts.

The origins of the Paris Conference reveal its purpose. It was convened, not to negotiate with the former enemy states, but to placate Allied opinion. Its purpose was to lend a semblance of democratic procedure to the process of peace-making. As Byrnes put it on 5th October 1945, 'the Unites Stated was willing to dictate terms of peace to an enemy but not to its Allies.'[1]

The Allies invited to take part in the Paris Conference were all supposed to have 'actively waged war with substantial force against the European members of the Axis'. Twenty-one nations were considered to qualify. As the Conference met, five political commissions were set up, each composed of representatives of the nations that had been at war with the enemy country concerned. Thus the United States, which had not declared war on Finland, was excluded from the commission for Finland. Britain was included, with five Commonwealth Countries (Australia, Canada, India, New Zealand and South Africa), in addition to the Soviet Union (with the Ukraine and Byelo-Russia) and Czechoslovakia. But although all of these had been formally at war with Finland, the degree of interest each had in the Finnish Treaty varied greatly. The war between Finland and Britain, for instance, had been unique in that it had reversed the current practice of making war without declaring it. Britain had ceremoniously declared war on Finland without ever taking military actions against her. The British declaration had been made in order to reassure the Soviet Union, just as Finland a little earlier had broken off diplomatic relations with Britain in order to allay German suspicions. 'If there has to be a break, let us do it in a civilized manner', Foreign Secretary Anthony Eden had said to the Finnish Minister in London.[2] It was so done; no blood flowed between the two nations; there were no hard feelings. As a consequence, however, British interest in making peace with Finland was as formal as had been the war between them. For the Commonwealth countries the Finnish issue seemed even more academic. As for the Czechs, in their eyes Finland probably seemed to be a remote country of no concern to them. In fact only one member of the commission genuinely qualified to deal with the Finnish treaty in the sense of having 'actively waged war with substantial force' against Finland, and this was the Soviet Union (including of course the Ukraine and Byelo-Russia). The Soviet Union alone had a direct national interest in the Finnish treaty and the power to do something about it. Its attitude was hardly likely to be much affected by whatever was said or done in Paris by, say, representatives of India or New Zealand.

Finland's political leaders were well aware of the futility of appealing to Paris for a change in the peace terms determined by Moscow, and the first point of the instructions issued by President Paasikivi to the Finnish Delegation at the Peace Conference was always to bear in mind that the maintenance of good relations with the Soviet Union had overriding importance and that nothing was to be done in Paris that might give rise to the suspicion that Finland was plotting with the Western Powers against the Soviet Union.

Yet the Peace Conference had a strong popular appeal. This was not only because in Finland as elsewhere in Europe there were people who having made war against the Soviet Union would have preferred to make peace with the Western Powers. To many the Allied gathering in Paris looked like a traditional peace conference of the kind that would draw up a grand settlement of all the disputes and problems left by the war, an international court of appeal that was expected to put right whatever was unjust and unfair in the post-war world. Prime Minister Pekkala did warn the public in a speech on 31st July 1946 not to expect too much from the Paris Conference and to keep in mind that Finland would have to continue to live next door to her powerful neighbour.[3] But his Government had to satisfy public opinion that they were doing their best to try to lighten the burdens imposed upon the Finnish people by the terms of peace.

The heaviest part of the burden was felt to be the loss of territory. The armistice agreement had reduced Finland in size by more than one-tenth; the pre-war population of the ceded areas had been 436,000, or 12 per cent of the nation. Virtually no one had stayed behind the new frontier; the Russians had taken over not scorched earth but land emptied of human life, a province of ghosts. In the aftermath of the Second World War, when millions had fled or had been forcibly evicted from their homes, the fate of the Finnish Karelians had received little notice outside the country. Yet there had been no parallel elsewhere to the voluntary and spontaneous exodus of the entire population of the province induced neither by persuasion on the Finnish side nor by force or terror on the part of the Russians. The manner in which the Karelians had been received was also unique. They had not been herded into camps but had been billeted, family by family, on the rest of the population throughout the country. And they were compensated for their loss of property, not only in money but also in land for those who were farmers. The resettlement and absorption of the Karelians, carried out without external assistance of any kind, placed on the Finnish economy an immense burden which it is almost impossible to calculate in money. But the social and political gains were equally incalculable. In a relatively short space of time, from six to eight years, the Finns who had lost their homes as a result of the war were re-integrated into society. As a consequence the Karelian issue was promptly removed from the realm of Finnish internal politics as well as Finnish-Soviet relations.

In the summer of 1946, however, the process of integration and resettlement was only at its beginning. The Karelians still felt keenly the pain of losing their homes. In the circumstances following the war the strategic arguments originally put forward by the Soviet Government to justify the conquest of Karelia seemed remote and irrelevant. With Germany in ruins and the Soviet power looming large across the European continent, was Karelia really necessary for the defence of Leningrad? In the weeks preceding the Paris Peace Conference Karelians held meetings throughout Finland, petitions were drawn up, and deputations visited Government leaders in Helsinki. No Finnish Government could have failed to forward the hopes of the Karelian people to the Allies in Paris, for the record if for no other purpose.

Presenting the Finnish case to the Conference on 15th August

1946, Foreign Minister Enckell said: 'It was understandable that in view of the great importance of the ceded areas the hope was being maintained that the final peace treaty would bring with it an alleviation of the territorial losses.' The Finnish Government, he said, 'sincerely hoped that the peace that was to be concluded would have the character of a reconciliation which would pave the road to an enduring friendship between the Finnish people and their great neighbour and form a firm basis for the independent life of Finland as a member of the family of free nations'.[4]

The Finnish Foreign Minister also pleaded for a reduction of the war indemnity imposed upon Finland. According to the Armistice Agreement Finland was to deliver to the Soviet Union goods worth 300 million dollars during a period of six years. The period of payment was later extended to eight years. It has never been explained how the sum of 300 million dollars had been arrived at. In the first peace talks in March 1944 the Soviet Government had insisted on reparations amounting to 600 million dollars, and this demand had been judged by the then Finnish Government to be impossible to meet. It took another six months of fighting to reduce the bill by half. But the sum tells only part of the story. At the Yalta Conference Winston Churchill had advised Stalin not to ask for too much in reparations, conceding, however, that 'the Finns might cut down a few trees'. But Stalin was not interested in trees, of which Russia herself had more than enough. He decreed that two-thirds of the goods to be delivered as reparations by Finland were to be ships, machinery and other engineering products which Finland had never produced in sufficient quantities even for her own use, and only one-third in timber and paper products which were her traditional exports. To meet this demand Finland had to double the capacity of her shipbuilding and engineering industries at an enforced pace. Since the prices of the reparation goods were fixed at the 1938 level with an increase of only 15 per cent in respect of machinery and ships and 10 per cent in respect of other goods, their actual value at current prices by far exceeded the sum mentioned in the Armistice Agreement.

During the first year of reparations, deliveries to the Soviet Union rose to 15 per cent of Finland's national income, and in the second year, to 11 per cent. To a nation crippled by territorial and other losses and exhausted by five years of war, this seemed excessive, especially when added to the cost of the resettlement of the

Karelians and the many other tasks of post-war reconstruction. It also seemed unfair considering that two much larger nations, Rumania and Hungary, were asked to pay the same amount. On such grounds Mr Enckell asked for a reduction of 100 million dollars in the war indemnity.

The Soviet reaction was swift and sharp. Foreign Minister Molotov, speaking at the plenary meeting of the Conference immediately after Enckell, rejected out-of-hand any possibility of revising the Armistice Agreement. According to Mr Molotov, the annexation of Karelia was still essential for the safety of Leningrad. As for the war indemnity, it represented only a fraction of the damage caused by Finnish troops to the Soviet economy. In a later statement on the question of reparations, Molotov advised the Finns to consider themselves lucky to get off so lightly. After all, he said, Finland, unlike the other former enemies, had no occupation costs to pay.

The main theme of Molotov's speech was to warn the Finnish Government not to attempt to exploit differences between the Great Powers. In private talks between the Finnish and Soviet delegations this warning was put more brutally. Molotov's deputy, Vyshinsky, told Prime Minister Pekkala: 'Just try to move the frontier closer to Leningrad with the aid of the Western Powers and you will see what happens to you.' He also said that any Finnish attempt to enlist the support of other countries against the Soviet Union would damage Finland's chances of obtaining advantages in direct talks with the Soviet Union. In fact the Soviet Government was opposed not so much to the substance of the Finnish proposals as to their presentation in Paris, and this line was echoed by the Finnish Communists.

Thus a reversal of roles between Finland and the Soviet Union had taken place since the end of the war. During the war of 1941–44 Finnish policy had aimed at localizing the Finnish-Soviet conflict, while the Soviet Government had made every effort to internationalize it and had indeed succeeded in persuading the British to declare war on Finland. When it came to making peace, the Soviet Government insisted on treating it as a bilateral affair, while Finland turned to the wider circle of Allied Powers. In Paris, it was Soviet policy to make it clear that the only way of gaining relief from the burdens of peace was to deal directly with Moscow. In fact, less than two years later, on the eve of the parliamentary election held in Finland in July 1948, the Soviet Government unilaterally announced a reduction of the Finnish war indemnity of almost the amount proposed by Mr Enckell in Paris. In the end the indemnity was paid on time – probably the only case in history in which a nation has voluntarily fulfilled an obligation of this kind.[5] On the territorial issue the Soviet Union has remained unbending, not so much because of the intrinsic value of Finnish Karelia as of the international implications of any move to revise the post-war frontiers in Europe. Years later, in 1960, the Soviet Government did agree, however, to lease to Finland a strip of Karelian territory along the Saima Canal which had been cut off by the frontier drawn in Paris. The Canal was rebuilt and modernized by Finland and reopened to traffic in 1968, thus linking the vast inland waterways of Eastern Finland with the Baltic Sea.

In view of the Soviet reaction the Finnish delegation to the Paris Conference omitted any reference to territorial revision from the formal observations they were asked to submit on the Draft Treaty drawn up by the Council of Foreign Ministers. They did include the request for a reduction of the war indemnity and added a number of other suggestions for revision. The military restrictions imposed upon Finland, for instance, were dealt with in detail. Finland's armed forces were to be 'restricted to meeting tasks of an internal character and local defence of frontiers'. The total strength of the army including frontier troops was to be limited to 34,400 men, the navy to 4,500 men and 20,000 tons, and the air force to 60 aircraft with a personnel of 3,000. Bombers and submarines were banned, as were nuclear weapons, guided missiles and torpedoes. Finnish military experts failed to see how 'the local defence of frontiers', considering the length of Finland's sea and land borders, could be ensured within the limitations imposed, and they asked for the maximum strengths of the navy and the air force to be doubled.

As important in the Finnish view as the material provisions of the Draft Treaty were some of its political clauses, for they seemed to touch upon the sovereignty and national integrity of the country. One of them, Article 6 of the Treaty, enjoined Finland to guarantee its citizens all democratic rights and freedoms. The Article had obviously been drafted for the benefit of the other former enemy states in all of which fascist regimes had been in power. In Finland, however, the rights and freedoms of the citizen had been maintained even in wartime to a degree that few of the Allied Powers sitting in judgement in Paris could claim to have bettered. To Finnish opinion the inclusion of such a clause in a treaty with Finland was proof at best of negligence on the part of the Allies, at worst of cynical disregard for the truth of the Finnish situation.

Even more dangerous seemed Article 9, according to which Finland had to arrest and surrender for trial all persons accused of war crimes and crimes against peace and humanity. This implied that it might be possible to demand that Finnish citizens be surrendered for trial by foreign courts. Such a procedure would have been contrary to the Finnish Constitution. The Armistice Agreement had left it to the Finnish authorities themselves to deal with those who had been guilty of war crimes and the Finnish Government considered that they had already fulfilled their obligation in this respect. Under Soviet pressure they had even tried and convicted eight leading politicians held responsible for Finland's entry into the war against the Soviet Union. This had been done under a special retroactive law of limited duration, a procedure that ran contrary to the most fundamental concepts of justice prevailing in Finland, and had been as repugnant to the judges as it had been to the accused. Both sides had played their roles in the trial in the spirit of national service, acting in the belief that such a sacrifice of principle was part of the price Finland had to pay in order to retain control of her own affairs. If anyone had to be punished for Finland's wartime policies it was better that this be done by the Finns themselves. The whole process had been accomplished with a minimum of bitterness. Finland was probably the only one of all the countries engaged in the Second World War in which the transition from war to peace was carried out without a single execution. The eight men who were held responsible for Finland's wartime policy were sentenced to prison terms ranging from two to ten years and all were released having served half their term. In the eyes of the majority of the nation they were neither dishonoured nor elevated to martyrdom. When former President Risto Ryti, who had received the longest sentence of ten years, died in 1956, he was given a state funeral, and President Urho Kekkonen, speaking at the graveside, stated that everything Ryti had done had been in the best interests of his country. Former Prime Minister Edvin Linkomies, a professor of Latin and Greek, became Rector of Helsinki University, and the Social-Democratic leader, Väinö Tanner, returned to Parliament and in 1957 was re-elected chairman of his Party. But in the summer of 1946 it seemed to President Paasikivi that all that the trial had been designed to accomplish might be destroyed through Article 9 of the Draft Peace Treaty and he instructed his delegation in Paris to request that it be deleted. He was also anxious to obtain a revision or modification of the final clauses of the Draft Treaty which set out the procedure to be followed for the settlement of disputes arising out of the execution and interpretation of the Treaty, for these appeared to confer upon the Allies the power to interfere in internal Finnish affairs even after the conclusion of peace.

The observations of the Finnish delegation on the Draft Peace Treaty, a document of eighteen closely typed pages, were at no time even discussed by the Committee dealing with the Finnish issue. The Draft prepared by the Council of Ministers passed through the Conference virtually unchanged. According to a story current at the time, the British delegate had asked his Foreign Secretary, Ernest Bevin, for instructions on how to deal with the question of the Finnish war indemnity and had been told, 'make a hell of a sympathetic noise'. But the story is probably apocryphal, for the British delegation accepted the Draft with hardly a murmur. This was wholly in line with British policy established at an early stage of the war when, all efforts to induce the Finns to stop fighting having failed, the British Government decided to yield to insistent Soviet demands and declared war on Finland in December 1941. From then on the question of Finland was no longer allowed to become an issue in British-Soviet relations.[6]

The British attitude caused a great deal of bitterness among some sections of Finnish opinion, but in fact it was more attuned to the wishes of the Finnish Government than was United States policy. The Americans did make a sympathetic noise on behalf of Finland in Paris; in plenary session they voted against the war indemnity and abstained on voting for the territorial clauses. But since the United States was not one of the signatories to the Finnish treaty these votes had no effect on the terms of peace; they may have soothed the American conscience, but they embarrassed the Finnish Government by feeding Soviet suspicions of Finnish attempts to enlist Western support.

In the end the Peace Treaty[7] was handed down to Finland off the peg, as it were, with no attempts made to tailor it to fit Finnish conditions. This outcome deepened the disillusionment of the Finnish public with Western policy and confirmed the lessons drawn by the Finnish leaders from the experiences of the Second World War. Before the war Finland had been hailed as an outpost of the Western world against Communist Russia. When the outpost had come under attack in 1939 the rest of the world had cheered and applauded its defenders, but no nation had hastened to their rescue. This experience had a profound and long-lasting effect on Finnish political thinking. As early as 1943, when the end of the war was by no means clearly in sight, Doctor Urho Kekkonen, then a Member of Parliament and later Prime Minister and President of Finland, pointed out in a speech in Stockholm that as a member of an anti-Soviet Western alliance Finland would always be in the position of an outpost which in the event of a conflict would be the first to be overrun, yet powerless to affect the issue of peace and war. He concluded that only a return to neutrality could ensure Finland's security after the war.[8] But neutrality had not saved Finland from war in 1939, because the Soviet leaders had not believed in Finland's ability or even her willingness to maintain it. The primary task of Finnish foreign policy after the war was thus to create a new relationship with the Soviet Union. The Peace Treaty which was signed in Paris in February 1947 was the first step in that direction.

IV. *1948*

THE MAN WHO WAS ENTRUSTED BY THE FINNISH PEOPLE
with the task of winning the peace with Finland's powerful Communist neighbour was a conservative, a former banker and diplomat,
with an impeccable record of opposition to the Communist ideology,
yet known to enjoy the trust and respect of the Soviet leaders. Juho
Kusti Paasikivi was appointed Prime Minister in October 1944, a
few weeks after the fighting had ended. For a while the Presidency
was retained by Marshal Mannerheim, the soldier-statesman, whose
immense authority and prestige had been essential to ensure an
orderly transition from war to peace. But in April 1946 the 79-year-old
Marshal, whose health was failing, retired, and Paasikivi was virtually unanimously elected President for the remainder of Mannerheim's term. In 1950 he was re-elected for a full term of six years.

Paasikivi, in 1944 already an elder statesman of 74, brought to his
office a lifetime's experience of dealing with the problem of reconcil-
ing Finnish national aspirations with Russian interests. He had
begun his political career in the early years of the century, at a time
when Finnish autonomy was facing the formidable challenge of
Tsarist repression. He had then joined the group of conservative
politicians who had been convinced that the national identity of the
Finnish people could be preserved only through prudent appeasement of the strategic interests and prestige of the Russian Empire.
This conviction never left him. In 1920 he was chosen to negotiate
the first peace treaty between independent Finland and the Soviet
Union and he was successful in obtaining Soviet recognition of Finland's historic frontiers; too successful, as he later was to point out,
in that these frontiers almost touched the suburbs of Leningrad,
thus creating a sense of insecurity in the minds of the Soviet leaders.
In October 1939 Paasikivi was chosen to lead the Finnish delegation
that had to face Stalin's demands, and it was against his advice that

these were finally rejected by his Government. After the Winter War he agreed to serve as Finland's Minister to Moscow, but as the German-Soviet clash approached he found himself increasingly out of tune with the spirit prevailing in Helsinki and he resigned a few weeks before Finland was once again embroiled in war with the Soviet Union. Throughout the war years he stayed out of office. Consequently, when war ended, he was untainted by association with Nazi Germany: he represented Finland's last reserve, at a moment when all other means of defending the country's independence appeared to have been exhausted.

Although the outcome of the war had in effect confirmed Finland's existence as an independent state, the foundations of her security seemed to have been destroyed. Finnish policy had been based on the assumption that the Soviet Union, combining traditional Russian imperialism with the Communist doctrine of world conquest, inevitably must aim at destroying Finnish independence. If this assumption was valid there was no hope for Finland. In the autumn of 1944 the balance of power in Europe seemed to have changed irrevocably. Germany was about to collapse. The Western Powers were allied with the Soviet Union; neither their interest nor their influence at the time seemed to extend to the eastern shores of the Baltic. Finland was alone, exposed to the overwhelming force of the Soviet Union. No wonder many people despaired of Finland's future, and some army officers began to store arms into secret caches in preparation for the inevitable last act of guerilla war in the vast forests of the north.

In this situation Paasikivi offered a new concept of Finnish-Soviet relations that not only was tailored to fit the prevailing facts of power but also was designed to restore the faith of the Finnish people in an independent future. He had always argued that the Russian interest in Finland was primarily strategic and defensive. It was to make sure that the city Peter the Great had built would be safe from attack through Finland. This, according to Paasikivi, was a 'legitimate interest', a subtle phrase which, like a shorthand symbol, conveyed both the direction and the limit of his policy of appeasement. It was designed to assure the Soviet Government that its need for security would be satisfied, while serving notice that Finland was not prepared to yield to demands that went beyond the legitimate – ideological demands for instance. By convincing the Soviet leaders that Finland would in no circumstances turn against them, Paasikivi believed, the Finns could secure their own independence and way of life.

Paasikivi may well have recognized his own thinking in what Winston Churchill wrote in his chapter on Munich in *The Gathering Storm*: 'Those who are prone . . . to seek sharp and clear-cut solutions of difficult and obscure problems, who are ready to fight whenever some challenge comes from foreign power, have not always been right. On the other hand, those whose inclination is to bow their heads, to seek patiently and faithfully for peaceful compromise, are not always wrong. On the contrary, in the majority of instances, they may be right, not only morally, but from a practical standpoint. . . .'[1] But in the late 1940s Paasikivi's policy was regarded by the great majority in the Western world as wrong on both counts. The prevailing view was that the Soviet Union was an aggressive, expansionist power which, far from being in need of security itself, was bent upon imposing Communist rule not only on the countries within its own sphere of influence but throughout Europe, by subversion if possible, by military conquest if necessary. Such a power could not be appeased, it could only be contained by force. True, Finland had not been turned into a Communist satellite, and to people with tidy minds this was an awkward fact that disturbed the pattern which was believed to underlie the chaotic flow of events. But it was explained away in a variety of ways: Stalin, it was thought, was only waiting for the Finns to pay off the war indemnity before striking; or possibly he was holding Finland as a bait for the rest of Scandinavia. Some even adopted the romantic notion that Stalin had a soft spot for Finland where in Tsarist days so many revolutionaries, including Lenin himself, had found refuge; but they failed to explain his lack of sentiment in ordering the attack on Finland in 1939. In any event, it was widely believed that sooner or later, sooner rather than later, the Finnish corner was bound to be tidied up.

And early in 1948 the moment seemed to have arrived. On 23rd February President Paasikivi received a personal letter from Generalissimo Stalin. It was short and to the point. Finland, Stalin pointed out, was the only one of the European neighbours of the Soviet Union with which it had not yet made a defence agreement against a recurrence of German aggression, and he wished to know whether Finland were prepared to conclude with the Soviet Union a treaty of mutual assistance similar to the treaties the Soviet Union had recently concluded with Hungary and Rumania.[2]

The date of the letter was significant. 23rd February was the day on which the Communist bid for power in Czechoslovakia was reaching its climax. World opinion was in a state of shock. When Stalin's letter to Paasikivi was made public a few days later it became inextricably linked in the minds of Western observers with the Communist *coup d'état* in Czechoslovakia. They were regarded as a two-pronged advance of international Communism upon the remnants of Western democracy in the Soviet sphere of influence. Once again, it was said, the smaller countries of Europe were being taken over one by one by a totalitarian power. The interests of the Soviet state and of the international Communist movement were seen to fuse into a vast conspiracy moving with perfect precision and co-ordination towards its goal of world domination. Stalin's stated purpose of creating a defence against future German aggression was dismissed as an obvious pretext. Germany, divided, occupied and disarmed, was in ruins: what was there to fear? The real purpose of the proposed treaty with Finland, it was believed, was to provide a legal excuse for establishing military bases or moving troops into Finland, not in order to repel German aggression but to destroy Finnish democracy. It was taken for granted that the Finns had no choice but to submit. Stalin's letter was regarded not as a proposal for negotiations but as a command to be obeyed. Finland as an independent state was speedily written off in the West. The Western powers could do nothing about Finland; but they could begin to organize themselves to defend the line west of Finland.

From Moscow, the European scene looked different. In the Soviet view, the Marshall Plan was primarily a means of restoring the strength of Germany as a spearhead of an anti-Soviet coalition. Having twice in a lifetime seen the Russian state come close to destruction through German aggression, the Soviet leaders were obsessed with the danger of a resurrection of German power. When Paasikivi in the autumn of 1939 had pointed out to Stalin that thanks to the Soviet pact with Hitler no danger to Soviet security could possibly exist, Stalin had replied: 'Yes, but everything in this world can change.' No doubt Stalin had the same thought in mind at the beginning of 1948: he had learnt from history to look beyond the ruins of the day. Throughout the 'thirties Soviet diplomacy had laboured in vain to induce Russia's western neighbours to agree to security arrangements against Germany; its objective, as described in 1938 by a Soviet diplomat in discussions with Finnish representatives, had been to make sure that the Red Army would not have to wait for the enemy behind its own frontier but could move forward as far as possible to meet him. The objective of Soviet diplomacy had not changed. During the war years, mutual assistance pacts had been concluded with Czechoslovakia and Poland. In February 1948 similar pacts were signed with Hungary and Rumania. Bulgaria was to follow in March. In retrospect these arrangements may seem to look toward the past and to be largely irrelevant to current conditions. But the same charge can be made against Western policies which were designed to meet a repetition of the kind of aggression practised by Hitler. If generals can be said to plan to win the last war, statesmen often try retroactively to prevent it, rather than to forestall future conflicts.

The timing of Stalin's letter to Paasikivi, therefore, arose from the hardening of the division of Europe and the beginning of the struggle over Germany, rather than from the internal events of Czechoslovakia. A defence pact with Finland had been on the agenda of Soviet foreign policy for at least ten years. It had been discussed in the secret Finnish-Soviet talks of 1938–39, and only after it had been rejected by Finland had Stalin made his territorial demands. He had not, however, abandoned his original goal. During the war the Soviet Government had asked the British as early as 1942 to give advance approval of its plan to conclude after the end of the war mutual defence treaties with Finland and Rumania.[3] The lessons of the war had only confirmed, in Soviet eyes, the need for such treaties. The Germans had after all attacked the Soviet Union through Finland. Reviewing, on 17th February 1948, the events leading up to the Second World War, *Pravda*, the Communist Party organ, said that 'the Finnish Government had declined the Soviet offer to conclude a treaty of defence and thus shown that the security of the Soviet Union was not safe from Finland. . . .'

In fact the late Andrei Zhdanov, then Chairman of the Allied Control Commission for Finland, had mentioned the possibility of a defence pact to Marshal Mannerheim as early as January 1945 and had raised the matter again with President Paasikivi in May of that year, and Foreign Minister Molotov had discussed it with a Finnish delegation visiting Moscow in November 1947.

Thus Stalin's letter of 23rd February was no surprise to the Finnish President. Nor could the idea of a treaty with the Soviet Union seem to him unacceptable in itself. The logic of his own policy impelled him to accept it. Having described the Soviet desire for added security as legitimate, Paasikivi could not very well refuse to co-operate in satisfying that desire. Indeed, he had said in a press interview in February 1947 that 'if anyone tried to attack the Soviet Union through our territory, we shall together with the Soviet Union fight against the aggressor as hard and for as long as we can'. Here in a nutshell was the commitment the Soviet Government wanted.[4]

But while agreeing in principle with Stalin's proposal for a pact, Paasikivi found the models offered wholly unacceptable. The Soviet treaties with Hungary and Rumania imposed on the parties an unlimited obligation to political consultations in time of peace and automatic mutual assistance in the event of war. Acceptance of such a treaty would have made Finland an ally of the Soviet Union in any and all conflicts between East and West, which was not the purpose of Paasikivi's policy of appeasement. If there is one dominant theme in Finland's foreign policy, it is the desire to avoid being drawn into the conflicts and controversies between the Great Powers and to this end to resist any commitments, not just to Russia but to any Great Power, that might fatally impair her freedom of action. Even in the winter of 1940, at the moment of their greatest peril, the Finns had preferred the Soviet peace terms, harsh as they seemed, to reliance on Anglo-French aid with its implication of entrusting the fate of the country to the Western Powers. From 1941 until the summer of 1944, while fighting on the German side, they had rejected every German demand for an alliance or other kinds of treaty commitment. And in the summer of 1947 they had denied themselves the comfort of American economic aid on the grounds that the Marshall Plan had become subject to a conflict of interests between the Great Powers. In February 1948 Paasikivi was determined not to throw away lightly the freedom of action that for so long and at such great cost had been preserved.

In this situation the Finnish President moved with majestic deliberation. Before making public Stalin's letter he informed the Government and the chairmen of the parliamentary groups. This took five days. On 27th February he sent Stalin a brief acknowledgement pointing out that in Finland a treaty with a foreign power required parliamentary approval and that therefore he first had to consult the representatives of the people. On 5th March he received the written views of the parliamentary groups. It took him another four days to appoint a delegation for the negotiations with the Soviet Union. On 9th March he replied to Stalin suggesting that the negotiations be held in Moscow. Another nine days passed before the instructions to the Finnish negotiators had been drawn up and approved by the President. On 20th March most members of the delegation travelled to Moscow by train, and its head, Prime Minister Mauno Pekkala, left four days later by plane. On 25th March, more than a month after receipt of Stalin's letter, the first meeting with representatives of the Soviet Government took place in Moscow.

The timetable of the Finnish preparations was eloquent in itself. It was an assertion of Finnish independence and a demonstration of the democratic process. The Finnish people were being reassured: their interests and rights were not going to be signed away by frightened men in hasty and secret deals. Parliament was fully consulted, not only before the negotiations but also at each subsequent stage. This is in accordance with the Constitution which says that in matters of peace and war the President can act only with the consent of Parliament. As Paasikivi put it, it was better to fail to reach an agreement in Moscow than to sign a treaty that would be rejected by Parliament. But the elaborate process of consultations also served another purpose. It fully displayed the strong opposition that existed in Finland to any kind of a defence treaty. Of the three parties represented in the coalition Government in power, only the Communist-dominated People's Democratic League was prepared to support the kind of treaty Stalin had proposed; the Social-Democrats and the Agrarian Party both declared their opposition to a treaty containing military clauses that might involve the country in international conflicts. Opinion among the opposition parties was even against entering negotiations with Moscow.

Much of the opposition was due to an unspoken scepticism with regard to Soviet motives. The post-war image of the Soviet Union as an all-powerful, malevolent giant made it difficult to accept at face value its professed sense of insecurity; the monolithic façade which the Soviet Union presented to the outside world hid from view the terrible scars of the war which explained its craving for guarantees against a renewal of aggression. But the Finns too were burdened with the lessons of history; all they wanted was to be left alone; any agreement suggesting the possibility of military co-operation with the Great Power that had been their traditional enemy appeared to most of them not only emotionally repugnant but also inconsistent with the neutrality that they hoped to maintain. Thus Paasikivi faced a double task, and it is hard to tell which part of it was the more difficult. He had to persuade the Soviet Government to be content with a security arrangement compatible with the Finnish desire to stay outside the conflicts between East and West, and he had to persuade the Finnish people to accept a treaty that would satisfy the Soviet desire for security on Russia's north-western frontier.

While three-quarters of the Finnish Parliament was opposed to a defence treaty, the delegation sent to Moscow was weighted in favour of the President's policy of accommodation. Its leader, Prime Minister Pekkala, represented the People's Democratic League, and it included one Communist member of the Government, Minister of Interior Yrjö Leino; Foreign Minister Carl Enckell and his Deputy Reinhold Svento, both of whom were close associates of the President; and three members of Parliament, of whom two, Urho Kekkonen of the Agrarian Party and J. O. Söderhjelm of the Swedish Party, also represented Paasikivi's views, and only one, O. Peltonen of the Social-Democratic Party, reflected outright opposition to a defence treaty.

On the other hand, the instructions the delegation received from the President were designed to ensure that any agreement concluded in Moscow would be made palatable to the majority in Parliament. Their chief purpose was to limit Finland's commitments to the bare minimum required to remove the historic Russian fear of Finnish collusion in an attack against Leningrad. Thus, the purpose of the treaty could only be to repel an attack directed against the territory of Finland or against the Soviet Union through Finland; Finland's role was to be confined to the defence of her own territory; and this defence was to be carried out primarily by the Finns themselves. Soviet assistance would be given only at the request of Finland or by agreement between the two countries, and military co-operation could be established only in time of war. The instructions also precluded acceptance of a general commitment to political consultations. The implications were obvious. As Paasikivi had said in the press interview a year earlier, the Finns were prepared to promise to fight against an aggressor who attempted to get at the Soviet Union by way of Finland and to accept Soviet assistance if they needed it. But they would promise nothing more. Finnish troops could be used only to defend Finnish territory; indeed, the Constitution prevented their use for any other purpose. If Finnish territory were not affected, Finland would accept no obligation to act.

After the alarms and anxieties, the rumours of pressure and the predictions of disaster that had preceded it, the encounter in Moscow seemed almost an anticlimax. At the first meeting between the two delegations, on 25th March, the Soviet Foreign Minister, V. Molotov, readily agreed to set aside the models suggested in Stalin's letter and asked the Finns to put forward their own suggestions for a treaty. The next day the Finnish delegation transmitted to Molotov a written outline based on Paasikivi's instructions. On 27th March the two delegations met for the second time, and again Molotov was far from intransigent. He accepted the Finnish draft as a basis for negotiation, and he offered no objection to its provisions limiting applicability of the treaty to the defence of Finnish territory. But he did amend the clause regarding Soviet assistance in a manner implying that in the event of an attack against Finnish territory such assistance would be given automatically. He also added a provision for mutual consultations on measures to remove a threat of attack against Finnish territory.

From then on the negotiations revolved around these crucial points. The Finnish delegation in Moscow was divided and hesitant and on 2nd April sent two of its members, Kekkonen and Söderhjelm, back to Helsinki to seek guidance from the President. The President once again consulted the leaders of the parliamentary groups, and on 4th April the two emissaries returned to Moscow with fresh instructions. These confirmed in essence Paasikivi's original position on Soviet assistance; military aid could be accepted only in case of need and by agreement between the two parties. They also limited the scope of possible consultations to measures against an attack itself rather than a threat of an attack. Paasikivi further insisted that the treaty include an explicit mention of Finland's desire to stay outside conflicts of interest between the Great Powers and that its duration be limited to ten years instead of the twenty years suggested by the Soviet Government.

The Finnish negotiators steeled themselves for tough talks. But they found themselves leaning against an open door. At a meeting on 5th April, Molotov gave way on all essential points. A final text virtually identical with the Finnish draft could be agreed upon without further delay. And on the following day, 6th April 1948, the treaty was signed in Moscow.[5]

An analysis of the key provisions of the treaty reveals that it closely follows Paasikivi's concept of the realities of Finnish-Soviet relations. Its first article states that 'should either Finland or the Soviet Union through the territory of Finland become the object of military aggression on the part of Germany or any Power allied with Germany, Finland will, true to its duty as a sovereign state, fight to repel aggression'. It further states that Finnish forces would be acting only within the limits of Finland's own boundaries and that the Soviet Union would extend to Finland assistance 'if necessary' and 'as mutually agreed between the parties'. Commenting on the treaty in a broadcast speech to the Finnish people on 9th April, Paasikivi pointed out that the first article really was a statement of the obvious: it described what in any case would happen in the event of an attack against Finland. 'We shall defend the integrity of our territory with all the power we have, and if we need help, we will get it from the Soviet Union in accordance with what will be agreed.'[6] The Constitutional Committee of Parliament later adopted the interpretation that any agreement on military assistance or military co-operation with the Soviet Union would constitute an independent treaty which would have to be judged on its merits with regard to possible parliamentary approval; on these grounds the Committee concluded that the treaty signed on 6th April 1948 accorded the Government no new authority beyond its normal authority to enter into negotiations with foreign powers.

The second article of the treaty dealt with the question of consultations. It states that the parties 'will consult in case there is found to be a threat of the military aggression referred to in Article 1'. In his commentary of 9th April, Paasikivi claimed that the commitment to consult had been defined in as narrow terms as possible. Both parties, he said, had to agree that a threat of an attack against Finnish territory existed before consultations could be held.

The other provisions of the treaty followed a more conventional pattern. Apart from re-confirming the undertaking contained in the Paris Peace Treaty not to enter into any alliance or take part in any coalition directed against the other party, the two signatories affirm their intention to act for the maintenance of international peace and security according to the principles of the United Nations, to develop economic and cultural relations between the two countries, and to base their relations on the principles of mutual respect for national sovereignty and independence and non-interference in the internal affairs of the other state.

Since the first two articles clearly contained the guts of the treaty, little attention was paid to the rest of the text, least of all to the preamble which appeared to consist of the usual phrases. Yet from the Finnish point of view the preamble turned out to be as important as all the rest of the treaty. It included the clause Paasikivi had insisted upon all along, stating that the treaty had been drafted 'taking into account Finland's desire to stay outside the conflicts of interest between the great powers' – that is, Finland's neutrality. True, at the time and for several years later, no explicit policy of neutrality was elaborated by the Finnish Government. The times were not propitious. Neither side in the cold war showed much tolerance to neutral nations; indeed, most small states were in flight from neutrality. Besides, Finland's aspirations for neutrality were at the time severely handicapped. Paasikivi did say in his broadcast on 9th April that according to the treaty 'Finland had in principle the right to stay neutral in a war between other states'. But he was bound to add that the lease of the Porkkala military base held by the Soviet Union by virtue of the Peace Treaty, as well as its right of free transit through Finnish territory to and from Porkkala, 'lent Finnish neutrality a colour of its own which did not quite suit the handbooks of international law'. As a clue to future policies, however, the neutrality clause in the preamble had a vital importance.

Why did the Soviet Government so readily accept the Finnish proposals for the treaty? It has been suggested that one reason may have been the change in the international situation that took place in the period between Stalin's letter to Paasikivi and the arrival of the Finnish delegation in Moscow. During those four weeks the Western world, shocked into action by the events in Czechoslovakia, had taken a long step forward into organizing itself against the Soviet Union. In the North, Norway was about to abandon its traditional neutrality, and even in Sweden defence measures were intensified. At the same time, though this was not then known to outsiders, Stalin's quarrel with Tito was coming to a head. The Soviet leaders could hardly have wished to take on more trouble in their relations with Finland.

Yet treaties between states are usually made, not in order to change relations, but to confirm and define existing relationships.

This was true also of the Finnish-Soviet treaty. It resembled closely the proposals made by the Soviet Government exactly ten years earlier and then rejected by Finland. Probably Stalin in 1948 had not expected to get more than what he had proposed in 1938. In any event he knew well that anything that had gone beyond what was finally agreed would have met with strong resistance from the Finnish Parliament. On the eve of the departure of the Finnish delegation from Moscow, Molotov even expressed some doubt as to whether the treaty as signed would be ratified in Helsinki.

The treaty was ratified on 28th April, by 157 votes against 11, with 30 absent, but the debate preceding the vote clearly revealed the reluctance and misgivings of the majority of members. It also echoed the internal tension then prevailing in Finland. Rumours of a Communist plan to seize power had prompted the President to order precautionary counter-measures. Troops were standing by, the police were alerted, and a gunboat was anchored in Helsinki harbour opposite the Presidential Palace. No *coup d'état* was in fact attempted and it is today impossible to say with certainty whether this was because of the precautions taken or because no *coup* had even been planned. The fact remains, however, that most people in Finland believed at the time, and continue to believe today, that the Communists did plan to take over power and that they were forestalled by Paasikivi's resolute action. This belief had a profound effect on political developments. One of its immediate consequences was a heavy Communist defeat in the parliamentary elections which were held in July that year and their subsequent exclusion from the Government. Even more important was that the rumours of an impending Communist *coup* provided Paasikivi with the opportunity to demonstrate in action that appeasement of the security interests of the Soviet Union could be carried out without giving in to the Communists at home. Paradoxically his anti-Communist stand at home gained him support for his foreign policy of friendship with the Soviet Union. Thus the events of April 1948 were a double triumph for President Paasikivi.

v. *Neutrality—Finnish Style*

PRESIDENT PAASIKIVI'S INSISTENCE ON LIMITING THE duration of the Finnish-Soviet Treaty of 1948 to a period of ten years was an act of statesmanship which, although it received little notice at the time, paid rich dividends. It meant that the treaty was to expire two years after the end of Paasikivi's term of office; as the moment of retirement drew closer, the aged President often pointed out to his associates that the first great problem his successor would have to face was what to do about the treaty: should it be extended as it was or ought an attempt to be made to amend it? But in the event it was Paasikivi himself who had to face that problem.

In the late summer of 1955, six months before presidential elections were due, Paasikivi received an unexpected offer. The Soviet Government was prepared immediately to return to Finland the Porkkala peninsula which in 1944 had been leased to the Soviet Union for a period of fifty years for use as a naval base, if Finland in turn agreed to extend the validity of the treaty of 1948 for another twenty years. Paasikivi did not hesitate to accept. In September he went to Moscow on an official visit and there, on the 19th of the month, the agreement to cancel the lease and to extend the treaty was signed. It was his seventh trip to Moscow in the course of sixteen years and the first one, as he himself put it, from which he returned satisfied.

The exchange revealed the importance the Soviet Government attached to its treaty with Finland, as well as its wary concern for the future course of Finnish politics. Obviously the Soviet leaders, too, had been speculating about what would happen to the treaty in 1958; and no one could be sure who might be elected to succeed Paasikivi. (Actually the election was decided by a margin of one vote in the electoral college of 300 members.) So they acted while Paasikivi was still in power in order to ensure the continuity of the policy set by him, and they were willing to pay a price for it.

45

Of course the return of Porkkala had also a wider international background. It was the time of the 'Geneva spirit' in relations between East and West. In the beginning of the year Nikita Khruschev had become the dominant figure in the Soviet leadership and he was giving Soviet foreign policy a new look. The Western Powers had been asking for deeds not words as proof of Soviet good intentions, and Khruschev was giving them deeds – first, in May 1955, the Austrian State Treaty, then, in September, the return of Porkkala. The latter concession also made it possible for the Soviet Government to claim that it had no military bases outside its borders (though it retained its garrisons in several East European countries) and to press its demand for the liquidation of all bases in foreign countries.

In the West, the return of Porkkala was generally dismissed as a cheap gesture. The base had clearly lost its usefulness. It had been the site of a Tsarist naval base and in October 1939 Stalin had argued that the Soviet Union, too, needed forward bases on both shores of the Gulf of Finland so that the entrance to the Gulf could be closed to hostile warships by coastal artillery fire, as had been possible in Tsarist times. At the time, Finnish military experts had vainly tried to convince him that his strategic thinking was out of date, and the experiences of the First World War had proved them right: once the Germans had taken the southern shore of the Gulf, the Soviet base in Finland, acquired at the cost of the Winter War, had to be abandoned. In the nuclear age the Porkkala base was even more obviously irrelevant to the defence of Leningrad. By giving it up, it was argued, the Soviet Union had given up nothing in terms of the global balance of power.

For Finland, however, the departure of Soviet forces from Porkkala in January 1956 was an event of profound significance. The existence of a foreign military base at a distance of just over ten miles from Helsinki had in Paasikivi's words 'cast a shadow over Finnish independence'. Had the Soviet Union had aggressive designs on Finland, Porkkala could easily have been used for pressure, blackmail or even a quick march on the capital. The fact that the base actually was never used for such purposes could not remove the anxiety or put an end to the speculation. So long as the Russians stayed in Porkkala, Finland was like a prisoner free on probation. Their departure meant in the first place release from the strain of living literally under Soviet guns. But the political implications of the Soviet concession were even more far-reaching. It lent powerful support to Paasakivi's thesis that Soviet policy in Finland was defensive and that his policy of prudent appeasement of Soviet security interests was the best way of securing Finnish independence. Obviously the Soviet Government had come to trust Finland to keep her end of the bargain struck in 1948 and no longer felt the need of keeping its watch at Porkkala.

The elimination of the Soviet base not only reflected a fundamental improvement in Soviet-Finnish relations but also transformed Finland's international position. There was an obvious parallel between Soviet actions on Austria and Finland in 1955. In the case of Austria the Soviet Government agreed to withdraw its occupation forces in return for an Austrian pledge of neutrality; in the case of Finland the Soviet withdrawal from Porkkala opened the way to international recognition of Finnish neutrality. So long as the Finnish Government could not claim full control over its territory it could not reasonably ask others to respect its neutrality in the event of war. The Finnish experience in June 1941 was a case in point. Immediately following the German invasion of Russia, Finland had declared her neutrality; but the presence of German troops in Lapland caused the Soviet Government to direct air attacks against targets on Finnish territory. Similarly, had war broken out between the Western Powers and the Soviet Union, until January 1956 the territory of Finland would have been a legitimate target for air strikes from the West. This was the peculiar 'colouring', to quote the phrase used by Paasikivi in April 1948, that the Porkkala base had given Finnish neutrality. Its removal was the essential pre-requisite of a credible policy of neutrality aimed at keeping Finland outside any future war. It was logical, therefore, that the Twentieth Congress of the Soviet Communist Party in February 1956, a month after the evacuation of Porkkala, was the first occasion on which Finland was called a neutral state in an official Soviet statement.

It was left to Paasikivi's successor to secure wider international acceptance and recognition of Finland's policy of neutrality. Urho K. Kekkonen, who was elected President in February 1956 and re-elected in 1962 and again in 1968, had been a strong and often controversial force in Finnish politics ever since the late 1930s, when he had first entered the Government as a representative of the Agrarian Party. As Minister of the Interior in 1938 he had banned the 'Patriotic People's Movement', a pro-German extremist party, as a subversive organization. At the end of the Winter War in March 1940 he had been one of the few politicians who had opposed making peace with the Soviet Union. But the bitter lessons of that war had later brought him to the conviction that Finland could not find safety through reliance on the protection of other powers against the Soviet Union. He had distrusted the association with Germany and had stayed out of office throughout the latter phase of the Finnish war, emerging in the autumn of 1944 as a leading exponent of the policy of friendship with the Soviet Union. In the Finnish-Soviet treaty negotiations in 1948 Kekkonen had played a key role, and as Prime Minister from 1950 until his election to the Presidency he had become closely identified with Paasikivi's foreign policy. Indeed, he was elected President primarily as the man best fitted to take over Paasikivi's role as guarantor of good relations with the Soviet Union, and in the eyes of the world this continues to be his role. Yet history may well judge him in less narrow terms. For under his leadership Finland has developed not only her own brand of a policy of neutrality but a new personality, as it were, in her dealings with the world.

While Paasikivi through force of circumstances had concentrated on improving relations with the Soviet Union, Kekkonen has ventured into the Western world and beyond. In the early 1960s he paid official visits to Great Britain, the United States and France, and in subsequent years extended his journeys to the leading countries of the Third World – Yugoslavia, India and the United Arab Republic.

As a result of his visits to the West, Kekkonen could claim that all the Great Powers had explicitly recognized Finnish neutrality. In Britain, Prime Minister Harold Macmillan expressed in May 1961 his understanding of Finland's policy of neutrality. President John F. Kennedy in October of the same year went further, stating that the United States would 'scrupulously respect Finland's chosen course'. A year later President de Gaulle made a similar pronouncement. In assessing the value of such declarations, their effect on public opinion is perhaps the primary criterion. In the Western countries they helped to dispel the widespread notion that Finland was a mere satellite of the Soviet Union. In Finland, where for twenty years people had suffered from a sense of isolation, they created fresh self-confidence and faith in the future.[1]

To the sceptical mind the Finnish claim to neutrality may seem as paradoxical as had been the Finnish attempt during the Second World War to combine waging war against the Soviet Union with maintaining good relations with its Western allies. How is it possible, it has often been asked, for a country which has a treaty of mutual assistance with the Soviet Union, to aspire to neutrality in the event of a war involving the Soviet Union? The answer is that the Finnish-Soviet Treaty of 1948, in spite of its official title, is not a treaty of mutual assistance in the ordinary sense of the term. It does not commit Finland to anything beyond the defence of her own territory. The question of obtaining assistance from the Soviet Union arises only in the event that a military attack against the territory of Finland has actually taken place – in other words, only if Finland's efforts to stay out of the war have already failed and her neutrality has been violated. In such circumstances a neutral state has the right to receive assistance from such powers as are willing to give it. And as has been pointed out previously, according to the Finnish-Soviet Treaty assistance is given only if needed, and its nature and extent would have to be determined by separate agreement between the two parties. In case the Soviet Union became involved in a war that did not touch the territory of Finland, Finland is only committed to refrain from joining an alliance or coalition directed against the Soviet Union – that is, to maintain neutrality.

An authoritative Soviet treatise on international relations published in 1957 concludes an analysis of the unique features of the Finnish-Soviet Treaty with the statement that it is in effect a treaty to guarantee Finnish neutrality rather than a treaty of mutual assistance.[2] The phrase is revealing. From the Soviet point of view the primary purpose of the treaty is to make sure that in the event of a clash between East and West, Finland will not abandon her neutrality by joining the Western forces or by failing to prevent them from passing through Finland on their way to Russia. The Western Powers for obvious reasons need no special safeguards to convince them that Finland will in no conceivable cirumstances join the Soviet Union in an aggression against them. The Soviet Union, for historical reasons, has felt the need for such safeguards. Thus, the Finnish-Soviet Treaty of 1948, far from being a handicap to Finnish neutrality, as is often believed, in fact strengthens it by making it credible in Soviet eyes. For the Finnish concept of neutrality, like the Swiss or the Austrian for that matter, is the result, and part, of a historical process, rather than the product of abstract thought; it is designed to meet the realities of power, rather than the precepts of international law; it is a response to the challenge of external circumstances which link Finland to the West with ties of history, ideology and economic advantage, yet place her within the scope of vital Soviet security interests and within the immediate reach of Soviet conventional military power.

While there are internationally accepted rules governing the conduct of a neutral state in time of war, there is no universally applicable guide to the kind of peace-time conduct most likely to ensure neutrality. Each country aspiring to neutrality must suit its actions to prevailing circumstances in order to convince the powers who matter of its willingness and ability to maintain neutrality in the event of a conflict. The crucial test is credibility. By this test, not only Finnish neutrality but the concept of neutrality in general has steadily gained ground since the 1940s. In the aftermath of the Second World War, most of the smaller nations of Europe abandoned their traditional neutrality in the belief that only the protection of a Great Power could deter a potential aggressor or, failing that, ensure that effective military assistance could be obtained without fatal delay. But the development of nuclear weapons and long-range missiles has brought with it a new appreciation of the advantages of neutrality. The balance of terror casts its shadow over all the countries of Europe, allied and neutral alike; in so far as it acts as a deterrent against the use of force, neutral countries benefit from it free of charge, as it were, just as much as members of alliances. At the same time the protective value of membership in an alliance has become questionable; for a small country it is coupled with the threat of nuclear annihilation.

While in time of crisis and tension neutrality requires a self-discipline that tends to restrict a country's freedom of movement, in a more relaxed international atmosphere neutrality has the opposite effect. It is in fact today just as much a way of life in time of peace as it is a preparation for time of war. As the former Swedish Foreign Minister Östen Undén once put it: 'In time of peace it is more satisfactory for us (Sweden) to stay unaligned than by joining an alliance indirectly to declare that we regard some countries as our potential and permanent enemies; neutrality in this sense suits us better and corresponds to our concept of normal intercourse between nations.'[3] Obviously neutrality in this sense also suits Finland, not only for reasons of security but also in view of her vital interest in foreign trade. President Kekkonen, speaking at the National Press Club in Washington in October 1961, described Finland's policy of neutrality by reminding his listeners of George Washington's Farewell Address, in which he had advised the young American Republic to 'exclude permanent, inveterate hostility' against particular nations and 'passionate attachments' for others, to avoid implicating itself 'in combinations and collisions of other states', to extend its commercial relations without political connections and to 'fulfil its engagements with perfect good faith'. These precepts, as Kekkonen pointed out, might well have been devised for the policy Finland has followed since the Second World War.[4]

VI. *The Best of Both Worlds*

TO SAY THAT THE TOUCHSTONE OF FINLAND'S NEUTRALITY is her attitude to the German question is to state the obvious. The German question is the great divide in Europe today. You tell me what you think of the German question and I will tell you who you are. But there is no obvious answer to the problem which the German question poses to a neutral country. There is no ready-made formula for dealing with the German question on the basis of neutrality. How indeed is it possible to maintain a neutral position between the Western claim that the Government of the Federal Republic of Germany is the sole legitimate representative of the German people as a whole, and the Soviet contention that there exist today two separate sovereign German states? To recognize the Federal Republic is to accept the Western claim; to recognize two German states is to side with the Soviet Union. Apart from the Soviet Union, which as one of the original occupying powers has a privileged position, only Rumania and Yugoslavia have so far established diplomatic relations with two German states, but the price they have had to pay has been tacit acceptance of the West German thesis that the Socialist countries of Eastern Europe had been compelled to recognize the Democratic Republic of Germany. This thesis is neither applicable nor acceptable to a country like Finland. Nor is the Finnish position in this respect wholly identical with that of Sweden. Swedish policy is defined as freedom from alliances in time of peace for the purpose of maintaining neutrality in time of war. Recognition of the Federal Republic of Germany is not inconsistent with such a policy. But Finland has adopted a more rigorous concept of neutrality by proclaiming her determination to stay outside the conflicts and controversies between the Big Powers, not only in time of war but also in time of peace. Neither recognition of the Federal Republic nor recognition of the existence of two German states would be consistent with this basic purpose of Finnish policy.

The dilemma has been solved by Finland in a manner that probably has no precedent in the history of international relations. Finland has recognized neither the Federal Republic nor the Democratic Republic; consequently she has diplomatic relations with neither. Yet Finland maintains trade missions in both and through these conducts business equally with East and West. By this device Finland has refrained from taking sides on the German issue without impairing her ability to protect her interests and maintain normal relations with both sides. Any attempt to fit this policy into the framework of international law would be a desperate undertaking. But in practice it has served Finland well.*

Finland's relations with the two parts of Germany did not come about as a result of abstract thinking or clever policy planning; they evolved over the years, almost imperceptibly, in response to changing circumstances; they had existed in fact for some time before they were defined in terms of Finland's policy of neutrality. In practical terms, the problem for Finland has been how to reconcile the need of a useful relationship with West Germany, one of her principal trading partners, with the necessity of allaying Soviet suspicions of any development that appears to indicate a resurgence of German power and influence in Russia's borderlands. Those responsible for Finnish foreign policy have never had reason to dismiss these Soviet suspicions, as is often done by Western observers, as a politically convenient pose. In Finnish-Soviet exchanges Soviet concern over Germany has not only been expressed with remarkable consistency over a period of more than thirty years, but time and again has also been translated into action, military and political. In 1948, Stalin was asked why he wanted a defence pact against the recurrence of German aggression: Germany at the time was in ruins, partitioned and occupied. He replied, as he had done in October 1939: 'The situation may change.' And it did. And in subsequent years, the two occasions on which Finnish-Soviet relations have become strained, in 1958 and in 1961, have coincided with international crises over Berlin.

Objectively, a good case can be made for the view that the Soviet Union today no longer need fear Germany. The actual Soviet view, a view shaped by tragic history, seems to be different, and

* Finland has also refrained from recognizing either side in Korea and in Vietnam.

that is the view that counts in the making of Soviet policy. In the light of history as it is read in Moscow, Finland has been part of the staging area of German aggression against the Soviet Union: in 1918, German troops were invited by the Whites to come to Finland to help defeat the Reds; in 1941, German troops were allowed to march through Finnish Lapland into Russia. The Finnish-Soviet Treaty of 1948 was designed to make sure that such things would not happen again. No Finnish Government could afford to ignore the implications of history as they are understood in Moscow.

Actually the history of Finnish-German relations is not so simple as it is usually presented both in Moscow and in the West. Of course Germany until the end of the First World War exercised a powerful influence over Finland. That is not surprising: Germany at the time dominated most of Europe. What is surprising is that at no time was Germany able to reduce Finland to subservience. Contrary to popular belief, Finland never was a German satellite. Nazi ideology made no significant inroads into Finnish political life, and such ideological demands as were made were consistently rejected. (Finland's Jewish community, for instance, was never molested, and its members retained their full rights as citizens throughout the period of Finnish-German co-operation.) Altogether, Finland succeeded until the very end to limit her political commitment to the German cause, thus retaining the essential ingredient of neutrality – freedom from alliances.

The Finnish policy of obtaining from Germany maximum military and economic support in return for a minimum of political commitment reached a dead end in June 1944. Faced with an overwhelming Soviet offensive on the Karelian Isthmus, Finland desperately needed military assistance. Now Hitler at last could insist on his pound of flesh: the price for German aid was a pledge by Finland not to make a separate peace. President Risto Ryti gave the pledge in a personal letter. Two months later, after the Soviet drive against Finland had been halted, Hitler found he had been paid in worthless currency. Ryti resigned, and his successor, Marshal Mannerheim, declared he was not bound by Ryti's promise. On 2nd September 1944 Finland broke off relations with Germany as part of the price of peace with the Soviet Union. The traditional friendship between the two countries sank to zero and then below. Contrary to Finnish hopes and expectations the German army in Lapland – a force of 200,000 men – refused to leave Finland voluntar-

*Finland's delegation to the Paris peace
negotiations in 1947. In the centre, Foreign
Minister Carl Enckell.*

*Signing of the agreement on the return of Porkkala
and the prolongation of the Pact of Friendship,
Cooperation and Mutual Assistance, on September 20, 1955.*

*President and Mrs Kekkonen being
welcomed to the USA by the late
President John F. Kennedy and Mrs
Jacqueline Kennedy. In the background,
Secretary of State Dean Rusk.*

*President Kekkonen on a hunting trip
with the Soviet Premier, Nikita Khruschev.*

ily, and it took more than six months of fighting and two thousand Finnish casualties to drive them out.

This was what military historians call a minor campaign, but for Finland and for the future of Finnish-Soviet relations it had a major political significance. To most Finns it was naturally distasteful to turn against their German comrades-in-arms; but they realized that if they did not expel the Germans from Finland, the Russians would come and do it themselves; having once entered the country would they agree to leave again? Clearly it was in the Finnish interest to fight the Germans without Soviet assistance, and that is what was done. Indeed, it became a cardinal principle of Finnish policy that whatever had to be done as a consequence of defeat, however disagreeable or onerous or costly it might be, was better done by the Finns themselves, on their own initiative and under their own management, so as not to give any grounds for outside intervention. This principle was followed in the war guilt trial, in the paying of the war indemnity, and in many less spectacular yet equally painful or burdensome cases.

Some outside observers mistook the Finnish attitude for subservience and an abdication of independence; in fact it was a defence of national freedom and independence. For national freedom and independence are not always synonymous with self-assertion or self-aggrandizement. According to Goethe, 'you must either rule and win or serve and lose'. For the Finnish people there had to be a third way. During the dark and lonely years following the Armistice, freedom and independence meant above all self-denial and a realistic limitation of national aspirations. Thus control over Finnish affairs at all times was retained in Finnish hands; thus, too, Finland gave convincing proof of her determination to live up to the obligations she had acquired through the Armistice Agreement. There can be no doubt that the Finnish effort to drive out the Germans, for instance, strongly impressed the Soviet leaders and helped to lay a basis for the new relationship of mutual trust that was to evolve between the two former enemies.

The fighting in Lapland was almost over when the Finnish Government finally got round to declaring war on Germany. This was done on 3rd March 1945, but the state of war between the two countries was declared to have come into force on 15th September 1944, the date on which hostilities had actually begun. This surely must be the only case in history of a retroactive or ante-dated declaration of war. The purpose of the declaration was to ensure Finland a voice in any future peace settlement between the Allied Powers and Germany, particularly with a view to presenting a claim of indemnity for the destruction of Lapland by the retreating German troops. At the time it was believed that the Second World War, like the First, would end in a grand peace conference at which all accounts between the belligerents would be settled.

In spite of the existence of a state of war, contacts with Germany were in fact resumed soon after the fighting had ended. Finland once again began to purchase urgently needed raw materials and other supplies from Germany. In 1948 Finnish trade missions were established both in Berlin and Frankfurt-am-Main; the former was accredited to the Soviet military authorities, the latter to the Western Allies. When, in 1949, the Federal Republic of Germany was set up in the three Western zones of occupation and the Democratic Republic in the Soviet zone, the Finnish trade missions in both parts remained and simply started to deal with the new German authorities. They continue to do so today. In a formal sense, the two Finnish missions in Germany have neither diplomatic nor consular status; in fact they perform all the functions, and enjoy all the privileges and immunities, of embassies. The same is true of the two German trade missions in Helsinki; the Federal Republic established its mission in 1952 and the Democratic Republic followed suit in 1953.

In practice, the policy of non-recognition has in no way hampered the development of normal relations between Finland and the two Germanys. The state of war was terminated by the Finnish Government in March 1954. Trade, cultural exchanges and travel are flourishing between the countries. The Federal Republic today ranks third, after Great Britain and the Soviet Union, among Finland's trading partners; Finnish exports to West Germany in 1966 amounted to 11·1 per cent of Finland's total exports and imports from West Germany to 17 per cent of total imports. The East German share was more modest – about 1 per cent of both exports and imports.

Naturally neither side in Germany finds the Finnish policy wholly satisfactory, but nor are they strongly opposed to it. To the Federal Republic, which has been recognized by the majority of the states in the world, recognition by Finland is less important than Finland's refusal to recognize the East German state. To the Democratic

Republic, which eagerly seeks recognition from outside the Socialist bloc, Finnish recognition would obviously be a valuable prize, and it continues actively to campaign for it. But in the meantime the East Germans make the most of the fact that Finland accords both German states strictly equal treatment, which they represent as a repudiation of the West German claim that Bonn alone is entitled to represent the German nation.

To Finland, non-recognition of the German states is more than a convenient way of evading an awkward problem. It lends powerful support to the Finnish claim to neutrality. President Kekkonen has repeatedly cited the Finnish position on the German question as proof of Finland's determination to keep out of the conflicts and controversies between the Great Powers. In a statement to the French newspaper *Le Monde* on 23rd October 1962, for instance, he said that 'so long as the German question remains an issue between the Great Powers, Finland will continue to adhere to her present stand'.[1] Many similar statements by President Kekkonen and other representatives of the Finnish Government could be quoted. Official Finnish statements have also referred to the Finnish Peace Treaty in support of Finland's attitude to the German question. Article 10 of the treaty commits Finland to accepting the validity of any future peace treaties or other arrangements that the Allied Powers might make with regard to Germany. This has been interpreted to preclude Finnish participation in any one-sided settlement of the German question; only a treaty made by all the Powers involved could be accepted by Finland.

A similar line was taken in the Finnish reply to the proposal for a German peace treaty put forward by the Soviet Union in 1959. The Soviet note of 10th January containing the proposal had been addressed to all the states that had actively waged war against Germany. The Finnish Government in its reply on 21st January agreed with the Soviet view that the absence of a peace treaty with Germany created an anomalous situation and that the conclusion of such a treaty would contribute to stability and a sense of security in Europe. Accordingly, the Finnish Government agreed to take part in a peace conference of all the countries concerned. The implication was clear: Finland would participate only if all the countries that had fought against Germany would join the conference. The note went on to emphasize the decisive importance of an understanding between the four Great Powers primarily responsible for settling the

German problem.[2] The reply was characteristic of Finnish foreign policy in general. Finland had replied in a similar vein to the Soviet Government's proposal for a European security conference in 1955: Finland would take part provided both sides in Europe were represented. Since only the Eastern European states agreed to the Soviet proposal, Finland did not participate in the conference which was held in Warsaw in May 1955 and resulted in the founding of the so-called Warsaw Pact.[3]

The Finnish Communists campaign vigorously in favour of Finnish recognition of two German states. They argue that failure to accept the existence of two German states is the primary cause of tension and instability in Europe; Finland, they claim, could strike a blow for peace and security, for herself as well as for all of Europe, by taking the initiative to break the ice, as it were, around the Socialist state of East Germany. But it is hardly likely that any such Finnish initiative could affect Western policy, while it is certain that it would weaken the credibility of Finland's neutrality and damage her vital commercial interests in West Germany. President Kekkonen, at a press conference in January 1968, rejected the idea of a change in Finland's German policy. He said he failed to see what the country might gain from such a change.[4] In fact, unless circumstances substantially alter, it is obvious that Finland has everything to gain from continuing her present policy. It is a policy that achieves something most countries desire and few ever attain: it ensures Finland the best of both worlds.

VII. *A Most-favoured Nation*

IN DECEMBER 1967 THE FINNISH GOVERNMENT ANNOUNCED that it was joining the Organization for Economic Co-operation and Development (OECD), an institution of 21 member states including all the countries of Western Europe as well as the United States, Canada and Japan. The announcement attracted little international attention. But for Finland it was a significant step, which can only be understood against the background of twenty years of Finnish efforts to keep up with Western European economic co-operation without formally taking part in it.*

About twenty years earlier, in August 1948, Finland had said no to the invitation to share in United States aid offered by Secretary of State George Marshall. The Finnish reply explained that Finland did not wish to take part in an undertaking that had become a subject of controversy between the Great Powers.[1] It was without doubt the most painful act of self-denial that Finland had made since the end of the last war. It probably put Finland's economic recovery back by about ten years and it may well be asked whether this really was necessary. After all, the invitation was for economic not political co-operation. Sweden accepted without losing her neutrality. But for Finland neutrality at the time was but an unspoken aspiration; relations with the Soviet Union were still fragile; and it was made clear beyond doubt that acceptance of the American invitation would have been regarded by Moscow as a hostile act. To the Soviet leaders, the Marshall Plan was not just an economic proposition; it was the beginning of the American counter-offensive in Europe; it was the first round in the Cold War. The Finns had to choose between the prospect of receiving several million dollars in aid and the credibility of the Paasikivi Line; a choice between prosperity and security. It is

* The exception is the General Agreement on Trade and Tariffs (GATT) to which Finland adhered from its inception.

59

of course futile to speculate how the Soviet Union might have reacted had Finland decided to choose the Marshall Plan. But the fate of Czechoslovakia may be a case in point. The Czech Government first announced its acceptance of the American invitation, and although it was quickly withdrawn as a result of Soviet pressure, the incident may well have fatally impaired the ability of the existing democratic regime to convince Stalin that Czechoslovakia would not once again turn against the Soviet Union. Six months later that regime was overthrown. At about the same time in Finland, President Paasikivi took overt military precautions against an alleged Communist plot, and a few months later the Communists were turned out of the Finnish Government, without reaction from Moscow. The Marshall Plan was designed to save Europe from Communism; Finland may have saved herself from Communism by saying no to the Marshall Plan.

Even in her relations with the United States, Finland has been able to turn her self-denial to some political advantage. Making a virtue of necessity, Finland has proclaimed a policy of not seeking aid from any quarter. This has added a new dimension to the image of Finland as the only country that has paid back its war debt. Now she is also the only country that does not ask for handouts. When President Kekkonen visited the United States in October 1961 an American newspaper described him as the only foreign statesman who had come to the United States without stretching out his hand – palm upward. And Secretary of State Dean Rusk said after his talk with the Finnish President that he was unaccustomed to visitors who did not ask for anything.

But the cost, in economic terms, was immense. Apart from the loss of several hundred million dollars in aid funds, Finland was excluded from Western European economic co-operation. The Marshall Plan was intended not only to provide aid but also to stimulate economic unity, and the countries receiving United States assistance combined in April 1948 to found the Organization for European Economic Co-operation (OEEC), the forerunner of today's OECD. Finland remained outside the Organization, yet Finland was part of the economic area it represented. By virtue of her economic and social structure and outlook, her standard and way of living, her tastes and aspirations, Finland is a Western country. More than most nations, Finland is dependent on exports, which account for more than a quarter of her national income, and Western Europe is the natural market for the bulk of Finnish export goods – the products of her forest industries. Unable to participate directly in West European economic co-operation, Finnish policy has had to employ a great deal of ingenuity to find roundabout ways of sharing in the continuing process of liberalization of trade. For instance, when the OEEC countries had formed the European Payments Union in order to free currency transactions between them, Finland founded in 1957 her own payments union, 'the Helsinki Club', to which all OEEC countries adhered.

Scandinavian co-operation at one time was thought to provide a possible back door to West European integration or even a substitute for it. During most of the 1950s Denmark, Norway and Sweden laboured to produce a scheme for a Scandinavian customs union, and from 1956 the Finnish Government participated in this work. In 1959 a plan for a customs union was virtually completed, and at a meeting of Scandinavian Prime Ministers at Kungälv, Sweden, in July that year, the Finnish Prime Minister declared that his government was prepared to submit the plan to Parliament for approval.[2] But it was too late. The plan was stillborn. It had been superseded by the larger plan of a European Free Trade Association – EFTA – comprising the other three Scandinavian states as well as Great Britain, Austria, Switzerland and Portugal. Its goal was to abolish within ten years customs duties on industrial goods and remove other barriers restricting trade between the seven member states.

The earlier birth, in 1957, of the European Economic Community of six continental nations (France, West Germany, Italy, Netherlands, Belgium and Luxemburg) had not placed Finland at a disadvantage in relation to other principal exporters of pulp and paper products, all of which stayed outside the EEC. With the emergence of EFTA in 1959 the situation changed radically. EFTA included both Finland's biggest customer, Great Britain, which buys up to a quarter of all Finnish exports, and some of Finland's main competitors in the British market – Sweden, Norway and Austria. British customs duties on most processed forest industry products varied between 10 and 20 per cent of value. Clearly Finnish exports faced a severe handicap if they continued to be subject to duty, while goods from EFTA countries could enter Britain free of duty. The demand for pulp, paper and board and related products was growing and expected to continue to grow rapidly throughout Western Europe, and with this in mind heavy investments had been made in Finland, partly financed with credits from the World Bank and other foreign sources, to expand and modernize the forest industries. No further arguments were needed to persuade the Finnish Government that it would have to secure for Finnish export industries the advantages acquired by their foreign competitors.

It had to be recognized, however, that the pattern of Finland's foreign trade differed in one important respect from that of the other Scandinavian countries. Roughly one-fifth of her foreign trade is with the Socialist countries of Eastern Europe, on the basis of bilateral agreements, the Soviet Union alone taking about 15–20 per cent of Finland's total exports annually. For the other Scandinavian countries, and indeed for all of Western Europe with the exception of Austria, trade with the Socialist group is much less important, amounting to no more than 2–3 per cent of their total foreign trade.

Finnish trade with the Soviet Union grew largely out of the war reparation deliveries. After the indemnity had been paid off the industries that produced reparation goods continued to find a market in the Soviet Union. Over the years they have acquired an established market, as it were, and are naturally anxious to keep it. From a national point of view, too, trade with the Soviet Union brings Finland important advantages. Finland sells to the Soviet Union mainly highly processed goods – ships, machinery, etc. – while the bulk of imports from the Soviet Union consists of raw materials, fuels, etc. Such an exchange clearly works to the benefit of Finland. Employment in Finland's metal-using industries depends to a considerable degree on continued exports to the Soviet market, while her balance of payments in relation to the Western world is eased through purchases of Soviet oil and raw materials.

In considering Finland's trade relations with the Soviet Union, the crux of the matter is that the exchange of goods must be balanced bilaterally and therefore in order to maintain her exports at the desired level Finland must also maintain imports from the Soviet Union at a roughly corresponding level. This fact weighed heavily with the Finnish Government in the latter part of 1959 as it prepared itself to meet the challenge of EFTA.

In a strictly material sense, the most serious problem for Finland was presented by the provisions of the EFTA agreement requiring member states to abolish quantitative import restrictions, in other words, the use of quotas to regulate imports. Without the quota system the Finnish Government could not make sure that Soviet oil, for instance, would be imported in sufficient quantities. As for the reduction and eventual elimination of customs duties on manufactured goods, the material effect on imports from the Soviet Union was negligible. Most raw materials, which formed the bulk of Finnish purchases from the Soviet Union, were free of duty, while agricultural products and fiscal duties were unaffected by the EFTA Treaty. Consequently less than one-tenth of imports from the Soviet Union in 1959 were subject to protective tariffs.

More important than the material effects, however, was the issue of principle involved. The Finnish-Soviet trade agreement of 1947 contained a most-favoured-nation (MFN) clause, a provision normally included in commercial treaties in order to ensure that the signatories will enjoy in their commercial exchanges benefits equal to those accorded to any third party. Accordingly, the Soviet Government was entitled to claim that, if Finland joined EFTA, any benefits accorded to the EFTA countries must equally apply to the Soviet Union. True, the General Agreement on Trade and Tariffs (GATT) recognizes the special status of free trade areas and customs unions with regard to the application of the MFN principle, thus enabling members of such associations to grant each other concessions without extending them to outsiders. But the Soviet Union was not a party to GATT and not obliged to waive application of the MFN principle in the event of Finland joining EFTA.

Several of the members of EFTA also had an MFN clause in their trade agreements with the Soviet Union. They all decided not to apply it with regard to concessions made within the free trade area; they argued, on varying grounds, that the clause had lost its validity or been nullified by previous actions of the Soviet Union; and they ignored the strenuous objections made by the Soviet Government. The Finnish Government took a different view. The validity of the Finnish-Soviet MFN clause was beyond dispute. Accordingly the Finnish Government declared that it would not unilaterally abrogate its agreement with the Soviet Union but would seek a mutually acceptable solution of the problem that would be created by Finland's entry into EFTA.

Thus the Finnish Government towards the end of 1959 initiated a complex process of negotiations with a double purpose – on the one hand, to persuade the members of EFTA to let Finland in on terms that would enable her to ensure continuity of her trade with the Soviet Union, and on the other, to persuade the Soviet Government to agree to a re-interpretation of the MFN clause. In short, Finland wished to join EFTA, but decided to do so in a manner that would not impair her relations with the Soviet Union.[3]

This Finnish policy seemed to many to suffer from a bad case of schizophrenia. Its two aims appeared irreconcilable. Members of EFTA understandably were reluctant to permit her to make to the Soviet Union concessions that might violate the very essence of a free trade area – its exclusiveness. To the more suspicious, Finland looked like a Trojan horse of Soviet make.

The Soviet Government on its part was adamantly and vocally opposed to EFTA. Obviously all such associations that excluded the Soviet Union and its allies had an adverse effect on Soviet efforts to expand trade with Western Europe. In these circumstances the MFN principle acquired a crucial importance for Soviet trade policy; it was the only means of defence against what in Soviet eyes was massive discrimination against Soviet goods. Besides, not only the European Economic Community but even EFTA were branded in Soviet statements as instruments of imperialist policy. Significantly, the Finnish Communist Party opposed even the opening of negotiations with EFTA.

It seemed, therefore, that Finland was faced with the stark choice of either joining EFTA and damn the consequences or staying out of EFTA and accepting economic decline.

But the essence of Finnish foreign policy is to avoid a choice of this kind. In the summer of 1960, President Kekkonen let it be known that he was prepared to go to Moscow himself to settle the problem of the MFN clause. He was saying, in effect, that he was willing to guarantee personally that joining EFTA would in no way alter the basic orientation of Finland's foreign policy. The Finns simply refused to accept the assumption that their desire to make a living in the world market could be incompatible with friendship with the Soviet Union.

The Finnish attitude, in a subtle sense, put to a test the Soviet policy of peaceful co-existence as it had been proclaimed by Nikita Khruschev. And Khruschev responded in person. Before Kekkonen had had a chance to go to Moscow, the Soviet leader himself arrived in Helsinki. He came in the beginning of September 1960 to attend Kekkonen's sixtieth birthday party. At the conclusion of the visit a communiqué was issued in which Khruschev conceded the main point in the Finnish case. The Soviet Government, it said, 'expressed its understanding of Finland's desire to maintain her capacity to compete in the Western market and agreed to discuss with the Finnish Government ways and means of maintaining and developing Finnish-Soviet trade in the event that Finland were to conclude a separate commercial agreement with the EFTA'.[4]

Several ingredients were needed to make that agreement and it is difficult to separate them, but obviously one of them was the personal relationship between the two statesmen. They met again in November that year, when the Finnish President visited Moscow. There a Finnish-Soviet treaty on tariffs was signed, to come into force in the event that Finland reached agreement with EFTA. In it Finland agreed to reduce duties on manufactured goods imported from the Soviet Union by the same amount and at the same rate as she was to reduce duties on goods from EFTA. But this concession was not made with reference to the MFN principle. It was based on 'the neighbourly relations' existing between the two countries. By this device the agreement was made palatable to all concerned. The Soviet Government could claim that in fact the MFN clause with Finland remained intact; the Finnish Government could claim that the concession to the Soviet Union had been made on grounds that were unique and therefore not applicable to any other state outside EFTA; the members of EFTA could similarly argue that the integrity of the free trade area had not been prejudiced. By some sleight of hand the agreement could even be fitted into the framework of GATT, if for no other reason on the grounds that many other equally eccentric arrangements have been allowed to stand without being challenged.[5]

An equally original solution was eventually found for the settlement of Finland's relations with EFTA. Finland did not join EFTA. Instead EFTA joined Finland. By a treaty signed on 27th March 1961, a separate free trade area comprising Finland and the seven member states of the original EFTA was created. In practice this meant that Finland acquired all the advantages of membership in EFTA as well as the right to keep in force certain quantitative import restrictions necessary for the maintenance of imports from the Soviet Union. She also obtained some extra protection for her agriculture and several branches of industry judged to be specially vulnerable to foreign competition.[6]

The successful outcome of the intricate negotiations lasting for close on two years had a profound political significance. It implied acceptance on the part of both the Soviet Union and the Western

Powers of Finland's position as a neutral country desiring to keep on good terms and to continue to trade with both sides across the front lines of the Cold War. The Soviet Government explicitly recognized Finland's vital interest in maintaining her trading position in the Western markets; Great Britain and the other members of EFTA recognized Finland's vital interest in the Soviet market. Either side could have pressed the Finnish Government to make a choice it did not wish to make. Adherents of the games theory in international relations may argue that they did not do so because neither side could be sure in advance how the Finns would choose. But to speculate about motives is seldom profitable. The fact remains that both the Soviet Union and the Western Powers preferred to accept a compromise that confirmed Finland's neutral position.

The economic consequences of Finland's joining the Free Trade Association have been equally profound. Customs duties on manufactured goods were abolished ahead of schedule; in the case of Finland, all imports of manufactured goods from EFTA became free of duty on 1st January 1968. Other restrictions on the free flow of trade have also been eliminated. As a result, Finnish exports to EFTA countries have grown steadily. In 1957 these countries bought 28·6 per cent of Finland's total exports, in 1963 the proportion was 31·2 per cent, and in 1966 it was 36·3 per cent. The corresponding figure in 1966 for the six EEC countries was 27·5 per cent and for the Socialist countries of Eastern Europe 18·7 per cent. On the import side, the share of EFTA in 1966 was 40 per cent of Finland's total imports, while 28·8 per cent came from the EEC and 19·8 per cent from the Socialist countries.

Increase in trade between the Scandinavian countries has been particularly spectacular. Finnish exports to Sweden, for instance, went up by close to 80 per cent in the five years from 1961 to 1966 and exports to Denmark by more than 80 per cent. Ironically, greater economic unity in Scandinavia, which in the 1950s was looked upon as a possible substitute for a wider European integration, has come about as a side product, as it were, of that wider movement. Now that customs barriers between the four Scandinavian countries have been removed as part of the removal of duties within EFTA, it is generally considered 'inconceivable', as President Kekkonen has put it, that such barriers could ever be permitted to be erected again. But to make sure of this the trade policies of the four countries must be co-ordinated to a greater extent than in the past. One step in that direction was taken in the so-called 'Kennedy Round', the tariff-cutting negotiations within GATT that were brought to a conclusion in 1967. The four Scandinavian countries were represented by a single negotiating unit, which in effect was a temporary supranational institution. This enabled them to face the EEC, as well as the United States, as a negotiating partner of considerable weight. The four Scandinavian countries purchase more goods from the EEC than does the United States, for instance; by combining their forces they were able to safeguard the interests of their own exports to the Common Market.

In their approach to the problem posed by the division of Western Europe into two trading blocs, the Scandinavian countries have followed different procedures. Denmark and Norway have followed Great Britain in applying for membership in the EEC. Sweden, too, has presented an application for negotiations, though with the reservation that she could enter only on terms compatible with the preservation of her policy of neutrality. Finland has made no such move. While British entry into the EEC remains blocked by French policy, there is clearly no pressing need for any action. But President Kekkonen has made it clear that 'if the systems of integration which already exist or conceivably could be formed in Europe can bring about organized co-operation with politically neutral states by arrangements which are favourable to all participants, then Finland's neutrality certainly does not hinder us from carrying on such co-operation in accordance with our own interests'.[7] With these words the President placed Finland firmly on a par with the other neutral states of Europe with regard to any future market arrangements. Obviously the emergence of a large market comprising both the EEC and Britain and the other Scandinavian countries would confront Finland with a situation similar to the one created by EFTA in 1959, and no doubt the Finnish response would be similar, too: it would be designed to safeguard Finland's vital trading interests in a manner consistent with her foreign policy.

In the meantime the four Scandinavian countries have taken a significant step towards greater unity in economic matters. The four Prime Ministers met in Copenhagen on 22nd-23rd April 1968, and agreed on a number of potentially far-reaching measures both on co-ordinating their countries' policies with regard to further European economic integration and on developing Scandinavian economic co-operation. They stated that all four Scandinavian states favoured the creation of a large European market and would work together to that end, while maintaining what already had been achieved within the European Free Trade Association. They also set up a group of experts to work out before the end of 1968 plans for closer economic co-operation within Scandinavia, including the establishment of a Scandinavian customs union with external tariffs harmonized with those of the EEC, as well as the creation of a joint investment fund and the gradual liberalization of capital transfers within the Scandinavian area.

The trend of lessening tension between East and West, and growing economic co-operation between the Socialist countries and the Western democracies in Europe, are likely to blunt the politically sharp edges of the problems of economic integration. As long as trade was supposed to follow the flag and economic co-operation tended to conform to the pattern of political and military alliances or even ideological loyalties, countries belonging to a bloc looked upon neutral states with suspicion or even hostility: the neutrals were accused of trying to get something for nothing. In today's Europe, where trade and economic co-operation are helping to break down the political and ideological barriers dividing the continent, neutrality is no longer a handicap for participation in economic integration, and it could be turned into an asset. On both sides of the dividing line the desire to restore European unity is growing stronger, and the neutral states have both the interest and the qualifications to promote such a development.

VIII. *From Honolulu to Novosibirsk*

THE YEAR 1961 OPENED WITH THE PROMISE OF TENSION and danger. On 6th January the Prime Minister of the Soviet Union, N. S. Khruschev, vowed 'to eradicate the splinter from the heart of Europe' – that is, to drive out the Western Powers from West Berlin. During his meeting with President Kennedy in Vienna in the early days of June, Khruschev delivered his ultimatum. Unless the Western Powers voluntarily agreed to make West Berlin a free city, the Soviet Government would sign a separate peace treaty with the East German Democratic Republic. This would automatically cancel Western rights in East Berlin. After that, any infringement of the sovereign rights of the East German Democratic Republic would be regarded as open aggression. Force would be met with force. Khruschev insisted he could not wait long, certainly not beyond the end of the year. He brushed aside Kennedy's warning that the United States would stand by its commitment to West Berlin even at the risk of nuclear war. In the following months he kept telling Western visitors that he did not believe the Western Powers would fight over Berlin, but that if they wanted war they would have it. On 8th July he dressed up in his old war-time uniform to announce a number of steps to strengthen the military preparedness of the Soviet Union. Kennedy countered on 25th July with 3·25 billion dollars worth of additional defence measures. On 3rd-5th August the leaders of the Communist parties of the Warsaw Pact countries publicly endorsed the demand for a solution of the German and Berlin questions by the end of the year. On 13th August the Wall went up, sealing off East Germany. American reinforcements were rushed up to West Berlin as a demonstration of Western determination to stand fast. The Soviet Government countered with an announcement on 30th

August of an extension of military service for certain categories of personnel. The next day it warned the world that it was about to resume testing of nuclear weapons in the atmosphere. On 9th September the disarmament talks in Geneva broke up. A week later the United States started underground nuclear tests. According to Arthur Schlesinger, President Kennedy estimated there was one chance out of five of a nuclear exchange.[1]

'It will be a cold winter': Kennedy's pithy summing up of his Vienna talks with Khruschev caused shivers throughout Europe.[2] In Finland, the Chief of the General Staff, Lieut.-Gen. Viljanen, briefed members of the Government on 12th August. He warned them that the mounting crisis over Berlin might soon involve Finland. The Soviet Government might well invoke the Finnish-Soviet Treaty of 1948 and request consultations on what ought to be done to meet the threat of German aggression. In such a situation, the General explained, the Finns could not convincingly claim that they had the capacity to defend their own air space. He urged the Government, as he had done many times before, to act without delay to enable the General Staff to build an adequate air defence. In September, a working group of high officials of the Ministries for Foreign Affairs and Defence and the General Staff was set up to study the military implications of the Finnish-Soviet Treaty in the light of prevailing conditions.

But the time for study had passed. On 30th October, the day on which the Soviet series of nuclear tests reached its awful climax with the explosion of a 50-megaton bomb, the Finnish Ambassador in Moscow was handed a lengthy note. It proposed 'consultations, in accordance with the Finnish-Soviet Treaty on Friendship, Co-operation and Mutual Assistance, on measures for the defence of the borders of the two countries against the threat of armed aggression on the part of West Germany and states allied with it'.[3]

The note claimed that West Germany had become a danger to peace in Europe. It was naive to imagine that West German ambitions could be kept under control within NATO. The fact was that the West German army had become the most powerful element within the alliance. West German generals, far from being controlled by their allies, were taking over control of NATO. They were demanding nuclear weapons. The Soviet note went on to charge that West German military activity in Scandinavia was increasing. The build-up of West German naval forces in the Baltic Sea was singled out as specially menacing. Denmark and Norway were falling under the influence of German militarism; they were in danger of becoming against their will accomplices of German revanchism. Even neutral Sweden underestimated the danger of West German military preparations, and Swedish industries helped to arm the *Bundeswehr*.

The greater part of the note dealt with the other Scandinavian states. About Finland very little was said. Some unnamed Finnish newspapers were accused of spreading a war psychosis and slandering the Soviet Union. But it was acknowledged that these newspapers were acting contrary to official policy. The Soviet note was an attack against West Germany and a warning to Norway and Denmark, and to a lesser degree to Sweden, against the consequences of co-operation with West Germany. It was not an attack against Finland.

This fact was largely overlooked in the first flush of surprise and alarm that the Soviet note caused, in Finland and throughout the Western world. Since the Soviet thesis of the German danger was not taken seriously, the idea that the Soviet Government wished to consult Finland on defence was looked upon as a transparent, even preposterous, pretext for putting pressure on Finland. Accordingly the note was regarded as a challenge to Finnish neutrality, if not a threat to Finnish independence. The Western press, once again, was quick to write off Finland as an independent nation. It was generally taken for granted that Finland had no choice but to enter into military talks with the Soviet Union, and once having done so, to accept whatever the Soviet Government had in mind. Speculation centred on what military bases in Finland the Soviet Union might covet. A Swedish newspaper sent its reporters to Finland's eastern border to make sure it would be first to record the entry of Soviet tanks. A crowd of foreign correspondents descended upon Helsinki; some of them had been there before in the winter of 1939–40; not surprisingly analogies with those tragic and heroic days readily sprang to mind.

By a quirk of fate, at that moment, the President of Finland was in the United States, in one of the remoter parts of Hawaii of all places, where he and his party were spending a few days relaxing after a three-week tour of Canada and the United States. They were having a picnic lunch on a beach when a telephone call from Helsinki was put through to a nearby hut and the text of the Soviet note was read to one of the President's aides. It was one of those rare moments of history in which the very veins and sinews of a nation's policy are laid bare as if by a surgeon's scalpel.

Through his visit to America – the first ever undertaken by a Finnish Head of State – President Kekkonen had reaffirmed his nation's traditional feeling of solidarity with the Western world. But his visit had also another, less obvious significance. It demonstrated his confidence in the stability of Finland's new relationship with the Soviet Union. Before turning westward he had to be sure that Moscow trusted Finnish neutrality. In his speech at the National Press Club in Washington, D.C., on 17th October, Kekkonen had sought to explain what he called the 'Finnish paradox' by saying that 'the better we succeed in maintaining the confidence of the Soviet Union in Finland as a peaceful neighbour, the better are our possibilities for close co-operation with the countries of the Western world'.[4] In Washington, President Kekkonen had had the unique opportunity to present the Finnish case to President John F. Kennedy and had succeeded in obtaining a public assurance of American recognition of Finland's neutrality. During his tour of the United States he had conveyed to the American public a new image of Finland, to replace the worn-out cliché of a nation forever heroically battling cruel Russian oppression or tragically enslaved by Communist imperialism – an image of a Western democracy maintaining its independence and freedom, not in defiance of its powerful Communist neighbour but in friendship with it. He had told American journalists that he was not upset by the lack of news about Finland: 'For we wish to stay out of the conflicts and controversies between the Big Powers and no nation that succeeds in doing so has much news value nowadays. The lack of publicity is indeed an indication of the success of Finnish neutrality.'[5]

But the Soviet note had made Finland front-page news throughout the world. The whole structure of Finland's international position as it had been presented by Kekkonen seemed threatened. That was how most of the world saw it. The President of Finland refused to see it that way. When he was asked later what he had done after receiving the news of the Soviet note, he replied, 'I went for a swim.' But before doing so he made a major decision which set the course he was to follow in the weeks to come. After a brief discussion with his advisers he rejected the idea that he ought to interrupt his American visit and fly home. He did order the Foreign Minister, Ahti Karjalainen, to return immediately. But he himself and the rest of his party were to stay and complete the programme of the visit as planned, including a stay in Los Angeles and the viewing of a landing exercise by an American marine battalion.

The message of Kekkonen's decision was clear: the Soviet note was not a threat to Finland, the country was not in danger. This was the theme of his first public statement on the note. In a speech to the World Affairs Council of Los Angeles on 1st November he described the contents of the Finnish-Soviet Treaty of 1948 and pointed out that the Soviet proposal of consultations did not introduce into Finnish-Soviet relations anything new in principle. Rather, it reflected the very grave tension prevailing in Europe. Kekkonen went on to re-affirm Finland's 'intention to remain neutral while maintaining the confidence and friendship of all nations', and he concluded by repeating what he had said a year earlier at a luncheon in honour of Prime Minister Khruschev – that he was convinced that 'even if all the rest of Europe were to turn Communist, Finland would maintain her traditional Northern democracy so long as the majority of the people wanted it',[6] as he believed they would.

Soon after his return to Finland the President, in an address to the nation on 5th November, pledged himself to defend Finnish neutrality to his last breath. He dismissed as absurd foreign press speculation about Soviet demands for military bases or pressure to change the Finnish Government. He advised foreign correspondents not to sell the bear skin before the beast had been felled. These words were designed to reassure the Finnish people; but they were also a signal addressed to the governments of foreign powers, including the Soviet Union.[7]

Kekkonen's two statements contained an analysis of the situation that differed basically from the popular view. According to him, there was no crisis between Finland and the Soviet Union. The crisis was between the Western Powers and the Soviet Union, and it was about Berlin. He accepted at face value the concern of the Soviet Government for its security. The note to Finland, therefore, was not a pretext for pressure against Finland but a reflection of the international crisis, and had to be dealt with accordingly.

But the President had also expressed in stronger terms than ever before his determination to defend Finnish neutrality. He had publicly dismissed the possibility of any military arrangements involving Finland. It was imperative, therefore, to find a way of reassuring the Soviet Government by political rather than military means. Acceptance of the Soviet proposal of military talks was clearly out of the question. It would have implied agreement with the Soviet thesis that West Germany was preparing aggression; the talks themselves, regardless of their outcome, would have seriously compromised Finland's neutrality.

This much was clear to all who were responsible for the conduct of Finnish policy. It was not equally clear how it could be accomplished. Of course, one way would have been to make a reply rejecting the need for military consultations. The Finnish-Soviet Treaty states that consultations are to be held in the event of a threat of an armed attack against the territory of Finland, or against the Soviet Union through Finnish territory. According to President Paasikivi's interpretation, both parties have to recognize the existence of such a threat. It could well be argued that conditions did not justify the holding of military talks. The Soviet note itself failed to make the claim, in the precise terms of the treaty, that Finland was actually threatened by an armed attack. It only spoke in general terms of the threat of war arising from West German policy.

But a reply along these lines would have transposed the international crisis into a Finnish-Soviet confrontation which President Kekkonen was determined to avert. In his speech of 5th November he warned the Finnish people not to allow themselves to be guided by the 'glow of outdated emotions and instincts'. In other words, this was not 1939. Kekkonen did not wish to have to say no to the Russians: he wanted to persuade them to say yes to Finland.

Accordingly the Soviet note was left unanswered. Instead Foreign Minister Karjalainen was sent to Moscow for explanatory talks. It was explicitly stated that his purpose was not to initiate military consultations in the sense of the Treaty, and no military experts went with him. Karjalainen had a meeting with the Soviet Foreign Minister, Andrei Gromyko, on 11th November. Gromyko explained that in view of the critical international situation the Soviet Government had to look after the security of the country's frontiers. For this purpose the Soviet military leaders had for some time demanded military consultations with Finland on the basis of the Treaty of 1948. Gromyko went on to say that his Government had full confidence in Finland's foreign policy. It could not fail, however, to take note of the fact that the political situation in Finland had become unstable. A political grouping had been formed with the intent of preventing the continuation of the present foreign policy. The Soviet

Government, therefore, wished to assure itself without delay that the present foreign policy would in fact prevail and that nothing would happen to disrupt the friendly relations between Finland and the Soviet Union. If this could be done quickly, then military consultations might be avoided.

Karjalainen replied that there were indeed different political groups in Finland but all of them were in favour of continuing Paasikivi's foreign policy. He said he was convinced that the Finnish people wished to remain on friendly terms with the Soviet Union. He then returned to Helsinki to report to the President and the Government.[8]

Karjalainen's talk with Gromyko brought to the surface an aspect of the situation that to many Finns, perhaps even most of them, seemed paramount. All nations are self-centred and the Finnish people need yield to none in that respect. Not unnaturally they reacted to the Soviet note of 30th October primarily in terms of their own affairs. And at that moment they were engaged in an internal political struggle of exceptional intensity and bitterness. A presidential election was due in January 1962 and a parliamentary election six months later. These were the uncertainties Gromyko had referred to. But to understand what he meant it is necessary to go back several years, in fact to the previous presidential election.

In 1956, Kekkonen, who was the candidate of the Agrarian Party, defeated his Social-Democratic opponent by a majority of one in an electoral college of 300 members. The campaign to prevent his re-election began then and there. His relations with the Social-Democratic Party became increasingly strained. In 1957 the Party elected as Chairman one of Kekkonen's bitterest opponents, Väinö Tanner, the man who had been the undisputed leader of the Social-Democrats until the end of the war and then had been sentenced to prison as one of the politicians responsible for getting Finland into the war. In Moscow his comeback caused deep mistrust. The Social-Democratic Party itself was split, and a minority eventually broke away to found a separate party which favoured co-operation with Kekkonen and the Agrarians and also clearly had the blessings of Moscow. In the parliamentary elections in July 1958, the disunity among the non-Communist parties made it possible for the Communists to emerge as the biggest group in Parliament, with 50 seats out of 200. The result shocked the others into agreement. In August that year, a large coalition comprising all the parties with the exception of the Communists and the dissident Social-Democrats was formed. President Kekkonen did not conceal his misgivings; he feared that Moscow would react unfavourably; but he bowed to the will of the majority and appointed the new government headed by K. A. Fagerholm, a Social-Democrat. Moscow did react unfavourably. The Soviet Ambassador was withdrawn and not replaced. Several negotiations on economic matters then in progress came to a standstill without an explanation. Trade talks scheduled to take place in the course of the autumn were put off. A freeze set in affecting virtually all aspects of Finnish-Soviet relations. As Khruschev later explained, the Soviet Government suspected that the new government, led by the Social-Democrats, intended to change the course of Finland's foreign policy. Finnish protestations to the contrary were to no avail.

The Finnish nation was deeply divided about what to do. Some believed strongly that the Government must stay, come what may, so as to assert Finland's right to order her internal affairs without outside interference. Others, including the President, considered it more important to regain Soviet confidence in Finnish neutrality. Then, as in 1961, there was tension over Berlin. If in a crisis situation the Soviet Government felt it could not trust Finland, Finnish-Soviet relations might deteriorate to the point of weakening Finland's own security. The President's view prevailed. In December the Agrarian members of the Government resigned, and the coalition collapsed from within. The President appointed an all-Agrarian minority Government to replace it. In January he went to Leningrad, ostensibly on a private sightseeing tour, but in reality in the hope of meeting leading members of the Soviet Government. Nikita Khruschev himself turned up to meet him. Their talk broke the ice. Relations were restored to normal.

Ever since, the Social-Democrats had been in opposition. They bitterly accused Kekkonen of having provoked, or even invited, the Soviet reaction so as to monopolize power for himself and the Agrarians. They were determined to prevent his re-election. In the spring of 1961 they allied themselves with the Conservatives and other non-Socialist parties to promote the candidacy of Olavi Honka, a retired Chancellor of Justice, for President. They insisted that their purpose was to put an end to what they regarded as a corrupt regime, not to change foreign policy. Once again they failed to convince Moscow. The Soviet Government looked upon Kekkonen as the guarantor of Finland's post-war course. In Soviet eyes he personified the policy of friendship between the two countries. In November 1960, Khruschev in his blunt way told a group of Finnish politicians representing all the political parties that 'whoever is for Kekkonen is for friendship with the Soviet Union and whoever is against Kekkonen is against friendship with the Soviet Union'.

This was what Gromyko was talking about when he told Karjalainen that the Soviet Government could no longer be certain of the continuity of Finland's foreign policy. Anyone familiar with the Finnish political situation was aware of Moscow's attitude. It was more difficult to understand how the Soviet Government could be reassured. Every political observer in Helsinki could have told Gromyko that Honka's chances of beating Kekkonen were practically nil; the Soviet Embassy had most certainly reported this. But of course no one could be sure until the votes had been counted. More important, the President, though possessing wide powers in the field of foreign policy, cannot alone determine the course of Finland's political development; Parliament, and the Cabinet responsible to it, are equally important. And it was impossible to predict six months in advance how the parliamentary elections might turn out and what kind of government would emerge.

In a democracy only the voters themselves can ultimately give a valid reply to the question posed by Gromyko. And Kekkonen decided on 14th November to let the voters have their say. Having heard Karjalainen's report he used his presidential prerogative to dissolve Parliament and order new elections ahead of time, on 4th-5th February 1962. Thus he shortened the period of uncertainty Gromyko had complained about by five months. His move also caused disarray in the ranks of the opposition. The parties supporting Honka had combined for the purpose of the presidential election only; in the parliamentary field the Social-Democrats and Conservatives continued to oppose each other. Now they were forced to conduct two mutually contradictory campaigns concurrently.

But Kekkonen's action failed to impress the Soviet Government. On 16th November the Finnish Ambassador in Moscow was called to the Foreign Ministry to be reminded that Finland had not yet replied to the Soviet note of 30th October. In the meantime, he was told, the international situation had further deteriorated. There was an immediate threat to the security of Finland and the Soviet Union. It was hoped, therefore, that a Finnish delegation would be sent to

Moscow as soon as possible for the talks proposed by the Soviet Government. What kind of delegation? the Ambassador asked. The reply was that this was for the Finnish Government itself to decide.⁹

Now Kekkonen had only one card left. He had played it success-fully after the crisis in 1958, and again in 1960 to solve the problem of EFTA. Once again he decided he would see Khruschev person-ally. The Government met on 18th November and asked him to do so. His request for a meeting brought the reply that the Soviet Prime Minister was on an inspection tour of Siberia but would be pleased to meet the Finnish President in Novosibirsk. Kekkonen arrived there on 23rd November and during the following day the two men had a long talk. Late that night a message arrived from Helsinki informing them that Honka had given up his candidacy in the national interest. But hours earlier Kekkonen and Khruschev had reached agreement. According to a statement released the following day, 25th November, Kekkonen had pointed out that the holding of military consultations between Finland and the Soviet Union was likely to cause concern and a fear of war in the other Scandinavian countries. On the other hand, if the Soviet Government were to withdraw its proposal, public opinion in Scandinavia would be re-assured and there would be less need for military preparations, not only in Finland and Sweden, but also in the two Scandinavian mem-bers of NATO, Denmark and Norway. On these grounds the Fin-nish President had argued that the security interests of the Soviet Union itself would be best served by abandoning the idea of military talks. He had also pointed out that in this way the Soviet Union would provide persuasive evidence of its sincere desire to practise peaceful co-existence, not only in tranquil conditions, but even at a time of serious danger.

Khruschev, according to the statement, had replied that he trusted Kekkonen's genuine desire to continue Finland's policy of neutral-ity, which had the support of the Soviet Union, and he had agreed to put off the military consultations. He had expressed the wish that the Finnish Government itself would watch developments in Nor-thern Europe and in the Baltic area, and if necessary would let the Soviet Government know what steps it thought should be taken.

The Novosibirsk statement, as Kekkonen later pointed out, had a far-reaching significance for the future application of the Finnish-Soviet Treaty and in particular its second article regarding consulta-tions. Paasikivi had interpreted it to mean that both parties had to recognize the existence of a threat of aggression before consultations could take place. This interpretation had never been either accepted or challenged by the Soviet Government. Now it had been in effect confirmed by the course of events: the Soviet claim that a threat existed had failed to trigger consultations. But the Novosibirsk statement went further. It suggested that it was up to Finland to take the initiative for consultations. This amounted to a reinterpretation of the somewhat ambiguous wording of the second article of the Finnish-Soviet Treaty in a direction that further strengthened Finland's neutrality.[10]

It had been a long way from Hawaii to Novosibirsk, but Kekkonen had accomplished what he had set out to do. He had succeeded in preserving Finland's neutrality intact. And he had done it, not by defying the Soviet Union, but by agreement with it.

Yet many people, in Finland and abroad, were puzzled and mystified. A tragedy is not supposed to have a happy end. Why was it that at the end of October the Soviet Government considered it necessary to have military talks with Finland and three weeks later agreed that such talks were unnecessary? It is indeed a mystery, if it is assumed, as it is often done, that good relations between a democratic, neutral Finland and the Soviet Union are an anomaly that sooner or later must come to an end and that the Soviet note of 30th October was meant to do the job. And then there are those to whom there is no mystery at all, for they view history as a vast conspiracy of evil men. They are convinced that the Soviet note and all that followed, including the meeting in Novosibirsk, had been plotted in advance, like a monstrous international charade, for the purpose of making sure that Kekkonen would be re-elected. But it is hard to believe that the Berlin crisis had been whipped up by Khruschev just to oblige his good friend Kekkonen. When the note and subsequent Finnish-Soviet discussions are examined in their international context, there is no need to look for either mystery or conspiracy.

The note to Finland was part of a sustained Soviet campaign, designed, as Khruschev later told a British visitor, to frighten the Western Powers to 'come to their senses', as he put it, on the question of Berlin. In retrospect it can be seen that the approach to Finland came at the climax of that campaign. Soon afterwards Soviet tactics changed. The shift was foreshadowed in Khruschev's speech on 27th October, at the end of the 22nd Congress of the Soviet

Communist Party, when he said that if the West showed readiness to solve the German problem, he would not insist on signing a treaty before the end of the year. Perhaps he thought his campaign had already achieved its objective and forced the Western Powers to re-open negotiations; perhaps he had realized that the United States really meant to go to war over Berlin if pressed too far; or did he already plan to strengthen his bargaining position by putting missiles into Cuba? One can only speculate. The fact remains that on 4th November the Soviet nuclear tests came to an end. On 21st November the Soviet Government agreed to resume negotiations for a test ban treaty, and a week later the three nuclear powers began their talks in Geneva. On 13th December they agreed on the composition of the 18-power Disarmament Committee. On 27th December the Soviet Government delivered a conciliatory memorandum to the Federal Republic of Germany. On 2nd January 1962, Foreign Minister Gromyko received the United States Ambassador to initiate a new round of talks, and that same day *Izvestiya* published a statement by Khruschev stressing the need for peaceful co-existence between the Soviet Union and the Western world.

Thus, by the time Kekkonen reached Novosibirsk, Soviet policy was already on its new tack, and Khruschev was clearly receptive to the argument that putting off military talks with Finland was likely to reduce tension in Northern Europe. In October Khruschev had been putting the heat on, in November he was anxious to turn it off.

Still, other questions remain, disturbing questions that go to the roots of the Finnish situation, indeed of international relations in general. Apart from its international context the Soviet note had a powerful impact on the course of Finnish politics on the eve of a presidential election, and the Soviet Government obviously knew it would have such an impact. The Soviet leaders never concealed their distrust of those who had promoted Honka's candidacy or their preference for Kekkonen. The effect of the meeting in Novosibirsk was to demonstrate that it was Kekkonen and no one else they were prepared to trust. But at no time did they attempt to impose the Communists on the Finnish people. They were not promoting a change in the internal situation in Finland; rather, they were anxious to prevent a change; their interest in Finland's internal affairs was defensive, not ideological. As Khruschev once put it, the Finns were of course free to choose whatever government they wished, but it could not be a matter of indifference to the Soviet Union what kind of government was in power in a neighbouring state.

Nor could it ever be a matter of indifference to Finland what the Soviet reaction might be. For it is a fact of international life today that 'the line dividing domestic and foreign affairs has become as indistinct as a line drawn in water. All that happens . . . at home has a direct and intimate bearing on what we can and must do abroad. All that happens to us abroad has a direct and intimate bearing on what we can and must do at home. . . . For, in a real sense, all of us, as individuals and as public officials, now belong simultaneously to a national and international constituency.' These words were written by John F. Kennedy (in his book *Strategy of Peace*,[11] 1960), but they could have been uttered by J. K. Paasikivi who never ceased to lecture his people on the need always to bear in mind that even domestic arrangements may have an effect on the world outside.

Paasikivi had learnt that lesson early. In 1918, when he was the first Prime Minister of independent Finland, the Western Allies withheld their recognition of Finnish independence until Finland had thoroughly purged herself of her association with Germany. Among the political leaders who then stepped down in the national interest was Paasikivi himself. And in 1945, the same man, again Prime Minister, urged the Finnish people to send to Parliament 'new faces' to replace those who had been identified with wartime policies. In 1918 and 1945, and again in 1958 and 1961, there was in Finland opposition to the course chosen. Time and again the Finnish people have debated, often fiercely and bitterly, to what extent considerations of foreign policy should be taken into account in decisions on such domestic matters as the composition of the Government. There are those who continue to hold the view that in 1958 the Fagerholm Government should have stayed on or that in 1961 the Soviet note should have been challenged. But the essential point is that at all times the decision as to what course to follow has been taken by the Finns themselves, rather than been imposed upon them by a foreign power.

On the issue raised by the Soviet note of 30th October, the final verdict was given by the Finnish electorate. After Honka's withdrawal there was of course no question about the result of the presidential election; it was expected that few people would bother to vote. But the unexpected happened. A greater proportion of the electorate than ever before – more than 80 per cent – turned up at the polls to give Kekkonen a two-thirds majority: it was an impressive demonstration of national solidarity. And in the parliamentary elections the turn-out was even greater – 85 per cent. One of the consequences of the heavy poll was that the Communists lost their position as the biggest party. This fact is the final twist in this story of paradoxes.

IX. *The Finnish Missile Gap*

IT IS A MEASURE OF THE RAPID PROGRESS ACHIEVED IN THE last decades in developing the techniques of making war that at the Paris Peace Conference in the autumn of 1946 the Finnish military experts, though objecting to several of the military provisions of the Finnish Peace Treaty, paid no attention to the one clause which not much more than ten years later threatened to prevent Finland from mounting even the limited local defence the Treaty was supposed to permit. This was Article 17 which prohibits the possession of 'self-propelled guided missiles or projectiles'. At the time the Treaty was drafted the phrase was thought to cover solely such offensive weapons as the V-1 and V-2 missiles used by the Germans during the Second World War, and the Finnish generals could not imagine that they could ever acquire, or indeed need, such things. By the end of the 1950s, however, the family of missiles had multiplied to the extent that its members had come to dominate virtually all aspects of military activity. Far from remaining exclusively offensive weapons, guided missiles had become indispensable for defence. Without air-to-air missiles fired by fighter planes or ground-to-air anti-aircraft missiles no country could effectively defend its air space against hostile aircraft.

And for Finland, air space presents the crucial problem of defence. In a conflict between West and East in Europe, it is hardly likely that either side might attempt to move large land forces across Finnish territory, nor do Finland's coastal waters offer scope for naval operations by the Great Powers. But it did seem possible, if not likely, in the late 'fifties and early part of the 'sixties, that in the event of war Finland's air space might be violated. The preservation of Finnish neutrality in any such conflict clearly required the creation of an effective air defence, so as to enable the Finnish Government to claim with reasonable credibility that it was capable of maintaining the country's integrity. The problem was that for this purpose Finland needed not only supersonic fighter planes to intercept hostile aircraft but also guided missiles with which to shoot them down, and acquisition of missiles was prohibited by the Peace Treaty.

The other countries which had similar peace treaties, Italy, Bulgaria, Rumania and Hungary, all members of military alliances, had simply ignored the limitations imposed upon their armed forces and acquired whatever weapons they considered necessary. That could not be the Finnish way. The Finnish Government at no time contemplated the possibility of purchasing military credibility at the expense of political credibility: Finland's security was better served by retaining the confidence of foreign powers in her willingness to abide by all treaty obligations than by improving her ability to shoot down a few airplanes. But it could be argued, and the military leaders did not fail to do so, that a conflict had arisen between the obligations imposed by the Peace Treaty and the commitments Finland had assumed through the Finnish-Soviet Treaty of 1948. In the latter treaty, Finland had committed herself to defending her territory against aggression by all available means; but the Peace Treaty prevented her from doing this effectively. Of course, the military provisions of the Peace Treaty could be revised, either by agreement between the Allied Powers and Finland or between the United Nations Security Council and Finland. But the reference to the Security Council had been inserted only in case the Council might wish to use Finnish forces for carrying out an enforcement action under Chapter VII of the United Nations Charter, and the Allied Powers were no longer allied and hardly likely to agree easily on revising a basic international document such as a Peace Treaty. Any proposal for a revision, however well justified or even uncontroversial in itself, would have reopened an East-West debate not only on that one point but on a number of related issues. It could not be in the Finnish interest to involve Finland in such a controversy.

In spite of the constant urging of the military leaders no serious effort to resolve this dilemma was made until late in 1961. President Kekkonen did mention the Finnish 'missile gap' to Prime Minister Harold Macmillan during his visit to Britain in May 1961, but at the time he was more concerned with another problem arising from the military provisions of the Peace Treaty. He pointed out to Macmillan, as he had done earlier in discussions with the Soviet leaders, that as a consequence of the high birth-rate in the years immediately following the war the Finnish system of compulsory military service could not be maintained in full force during some years in the 1960s without exceeding by a few thousand the manpower limitations imposed by the Peace Treaty. Kekkonen asked the Soviet and British Governments, as principal signatories of the treaty, to ignore such technical infractions of the treaty provisions, and that is what actually happened.

It could hardly matter either to the Soviet Union or to the Western Powers whether Finland at any given moment has 41,900 men in uniform, as stipulated by the Peace Treaty, or a few thousand more. The question of missiles was of a different order, politically as well as militarily. The urgency of settling it was finally brought home by the Berlin crisis in 1961. Had the crisis developed into an acute military confrontation between East and West with an immediate danger of war, the Finnish Government could have been exposed to the charge that it was incapable of preventing foreign powers from using the air space over Finland with impunity. Realization of the dangerous implications of such a situation jolted the Government into action.

The first step was to send, in January 1962, a purchasing mission to Moscow with a shopping list that included MIG 21-type fighter planes with air-to-air missiles as well as ground-to-air anti-aircraft missiles. The Soviet authorities quickly agreed to sell the equipment the Finns had asked for, and the contracts were duly completed. But with regard to the missiles the deal was left in suspense, as it were, until the other signatories of the Peace Treaty could be persuaded to agree that Finland was entitled to acquire such weapons. In the meantime no missiles were to be delivered. Great Britain as the principal Western signatory was tackled first. In view of the obvious difficulties in the way of obtaining a formal revision of the treaty, a more gentle line of approach was chosen. The Finnish Government suggested that, in the light of the technical developments that had taken place since 1947 Article 17 of the treaty should be re-interpreted in a manner that would permit Finland to acquire guided missiles for defensive purposes. This, it was argued, could not be contrary to the spirit and the purpose of the treaty. Its military provisions, designed to prevent Finland from developing an offensive military capability, stated that Finland's armed forces must be limited to the local defence of her borders. But without defensive guided missiles even such a limited task could no longer be carried out. Thus the treaty could be said to deprive Finland of her inherent right to self-defence under the Charter of the United Nations.

The unorthodox idea of re-interpreting the Peace Treaty without actually revising it encountered initially some doubt and suspicion. But after some months of negotiation, in October 1962, the British Government accepted it, acting on the assumption that Finland would continue to adhere to her established practice of directing purchases of sensitive military equipment in a manner consistent with her policy of neutrality, or to put it more plainly, keeping a balance between purchases from East and West. (For instance, the Finnish Air Force consists of planes from Britain, France and the Soviet Union; radar equipment has been bought from Britain; naval craft from the Soviet Union and Britain.) By the end of the year the consent of the other signatories of the Peace Treaties was obtained. The Finnish Government then quickly consummated the agreement by confirming its order for Soviet air-to-air missiles and balancing this with the purchase of anti-tank missiles from Britain. A statement made public on 9th January 1963 revealed for the first time that agreement had been reached with the signatories of the Peace Treaty to the effect of permitting Finland to acquire defensive guided missiles.[1]

The agreement removed the legal obstacles in the way of creating an effective air defence. Financial obstacles remained and have slowed down the execution of the original plans of the military leaders. Ground-to-air missiles, for instance, were not actually purchased. But apart from its material effect, the agreement to re-interpret the Peace Treaty could be presented as a valuable political prize. As was pointed out in the official statement of 9th January 1963, the fact that both the Soviet Union and Great Britain had accepted the Finnish proposal was 'a significant expression of confidence in Finland's policy of neutrality'. At one time during the negotiations a high Western official had asked: 'Against whom does Finland need these weapons?' The answer was that Finland did not point her guns against anyone: they were needed solely for the defence of Finnish neutrality. By agreeing to sell Finland fighters and missiles both sides in the Cold War implicitly recognized the validity of that answer.

In Finland the closing of the missile gap had an additional political impact: it directed attention to the new role of the armed forces as an integral element of a policy of neutrality. Until that time there had been almost no public debate and very little private thinking on the question of what the function of the armed forces ought to be in the strange new world of nuclear deterrence and counter-deterrence. In earlier days, before September 1944, the answer had been self-evident: the armed forces were there to defend the country against invasion from the East. Most Finnish men who had grown up during the 1920s and 1930s had taken it for granted that sooner or later they would be called upon to take up arms to fight the Russians. In the changed circumstances of the post-war era the traditional defence philosophy was neither politically appropriate nor militarily feasible. But for more than a decade no real effort was made to replace it with a more modern concept. There did not really seem to be one that would make sense. As a result the armed forces seemed to lead a pointless existence, like an ancient institution that no longer has any practical function to perform, yet is maintained for sentimental reasons. They did continue to train the yearly crop of conscripts; they were not granted enough resources to do much more.

Much of the sense of futility as well as the sentimental attachments that coloured popular attitudes to the question of defence could be traced to the powerful influence exercised by the memories of the Winter War of 1939–40. Nothing could be further from the truth than Hegel's well-known contention that 'peoples and governments never have learned anything from history or acted on principles deduced from it'. A more valid generalization is to say that peoples and governments tend to cling far too rigidly to what they regard as the lessons of history. The Winter War was one of those traumatic events that contribute to the political mythology of a nation. It was a triumph of the Finnish will to survive; it also meant the failure of the pre-war policy of neutrality. It could be held up as evidence that even a small nation can successfully defend itself; but it was also proof of the opposite. To many Finns, the lessons of the War, both the triumph and the tragedy, were summed up by a character in a popular war novel when he said 'one Finn may be worth ten Russians, but what do we do when the eleventh comes along?' Yet this view of the Winter War as a duel between David and Goliath fought out in a vacuum, as it were, was an optical illusion. The origins of the War as well as its conclusion can only be understood in the wider context of the Second World War: that eleventh Russian was guarding his country's other frontiers.

D

In today's conditions it is even more unreal to assess Finland's defence capacity in relation to the military strength of a great power, as if her security depended on ability to fight another Winter War. For the real lesson of that war is that it was a unique historical event which has no relevance to present-day circumstances. The invasion of Finland was an aberration of Soviet policy from its normal pattern of behaviour, and the strategic considerations that prompted it are closer to the thinking of Peter the Great than to present military concepts. Tsar Peter had said that the ladies of St Petersburg could not sleep in peace so long as the Finnish border – that is, the border of the Swedish empire – was so close to the city as it then was. Stalin spoke in similar terms when in 1939 he complained that Leningrad could be shelled by artillery from behind the Finnish border. Today's artillery – the ballistic missile – can devastate Leningrad from behind the Atlantic Ocean. The added defensive depth provided by a few hundred miles of Finnish territory would no longer make any difference, not even for the effectiveness of radar or anti-missile missiles. Accordingly, as was pointed out by President Kekkonen in a speech on 29th November 1965, 'Finland and the entire Scandinavian region have less strategic value to the Great Powers than before'. He went on to point out that offensive action that used to require the movement of armies, navies and aircraft could now be initiated with missiles fired from far away, while defensive measures had to be concentrated to the immediate vicinity of the target area. 'The value of defensive buffer areas has thus been considerably reduced. Single military bases or territorial questions in the strict sense of the phrase have no longer the importance they used to have.' Altogether, he went on, there was less likelihood of a general war, nor was it likely that limited wars could occur in Europe where they could easily escalate into conflicts between the Great Powers. All this, the President said,[2] had eased Finland's military situation. And on the occasion of Finland's fiftieth anniversary of independence, on 6th December 1967, Kekkonen declared that the security of the country had never been greater.

Obviously, it is not security based on military power. Finland spends only about 1·6 per cent of her gross national product on defence – proportionately less than any other state in Europe. It is security based primarily on a policy designed to keep Finland out of war. But the armed forces still retain an important supporting role. Since it is inconceivable that any power would attack Finland for her own sake, in a separate local action, the danger of Finland's becoming involved in military operations arises only in a general European conflict or in a situation in which such a conflict is considered imminent. Even then Finland, situated as she is well off the centre of the stage, would have a better chance of maintaining her neutrality than most countries on the continent. Yet so long as the long-range bomber has not been scrapped as obsolete, the danger of overflights could not be ruled out. In theory at least, the North Cap, as the northernmost top of the Scandinavian Peninsula is called, where the territories of Finland and Norway touch the Soviet Union, could also become the scene of a clash between NATO and Soviet forces. And the Soviet leaders, in spite of their mastery of the most sophisticated weapons systems, tend to adhere to the traditional concept of national security as maximum defensive capability against all possible forms of attack along all the borders of their vast country. In a revealing remark to a Scandinavian visitor, the late Defence Minister Marshal Malinovski once pointed out that thanks to Finland's friendly neutrality only one Soviet division had to be maintained in the Murmansk region; if Finnish policy were different, he said, much greater forces would have to be kept there. No doubt he would draw the same conclusion if Finland were a military vacuum. The Soviet Marshals might then consider it necessary in a critical situation to move their defence forward into that vacuum. Such a move, apart from any other possible consequences, would immediately destroy Finland's chances of staying outside the conflict. It is therefore a paramount Finnish interest to maintain a credible defensive capability. Since its potential use would be confined to an area which in no circumstances could have more than secondary importance, and to a situation in which the resources of even great powers would be stretched to the utmost, such a capability can be achieved with relatively modest means.

This much is generally accepted in Finland today. There is less agreement on what could be considered a reasonable and sufficient degree of military preparedness. Air defence, for instance, though qualitatively and quantitatively much improved since 1961, is not yet on the level that the military leaders consider adequate. The army continues to follow its traditional policy of training conscripts and thus maintaining large reserves. Finland could in fact mobilize more than 700,000 men. Yet it might be more useful to devote a greater proportion of the limited resources available to maintaining highly mobile forces in readiness as a precaution against surprise attack, which has been accorded high priority in defence planning. It would be premature, therefore, to claim that Finland's armed forces were as yet adequate for their new role. But it can be said that Finland is moving toward a more sophisticated defence policy designed to support her policy of neutrality in moments of international crisis.

X. *The Scandinavian Balance*

THE SCANDINAVIAN NATIONS,* THOUGH FORMALLY SEP-
arated in matters of security, in fact live today in a state of greater
interdependence than ever before. This has rarely been so vividly
illustrated as in the Finnish-Soviet dialogue that took place in
October and November 1961: first, in the Soviet note to Finland
which claimed that the alleged increase of West German military
activity in Norway and Denmark required military countermeasures
on the part of both Finland and the Soviet Union; then, in the talks
in Novosibirsk, where President Kekkonen was able to persuade
Khruschev to accept the view that such countermeasures would only
alarm the other Scandinavian countries and cause an intensification
of military activities on their territories, whereas a Soviet reaffirma-
tion of respect for Finnish neutrality would tend to relax them and
thus remove any threat to Soviet security.

The interdependence is obvious, its precise nature less so. It is
sometimes suggested, for instance, that Sweden has stayed neutral in
order to 'save Finland', as it were, from a closer alignment with the
Soviet Union. It would make as much, or rather, as little sense to
claim that Finland fought to retain her independence in order to
make it easier for Sweden to stay neutral. The fact is that not even
the Soviet invasion of Finland in 1939 induced Sweden to abandon
her neutrality. After the Second World War, Sweden continued her
traditional policy because it had kept the country out of war for
more than 150 years and, as former Foreign Minister Östen Undén
has put it, public opinion would not have gone along with any
change of course. But motives count less than the actual effects
and consequences of policies pursued. Obviously the continued

* Throughout this book I have used the term 'Scandinavian' rather than
'Nordic' to denote the group of countries comprising Denmark, Finland,
Iceland, Norway and Sweden.

neutrality of Sweden has helped Finland to develop her own policy of neutrality by removing most of Finland's borders from the line of direct military confrontation between the alliances of East and West. Neutral Finland has rendered Sweden a similar service. Today the two countries, pursuing independently parallel policies, mutually support each other's positions. At the same time, the restraint practised by Denmark and Norway as members of NATO in refusing to permit the stationing of foreign armed forces or nuclear weapons on their soil in time of peace has had the effect of reducing to a minimum the military presence of outside powers in the Scandinavian area. Thus the four Scandinavian states, while each looks after its own security in accordance with its own circumstances and historical experience, in effect have combined to create a semi-neutral, semi-detached region – neither wholly neutral nor unequivocally aligned – that by and large has remained outside the immediate range of international tensions.

From this a theory of a 'Scandinavian balance' has been constructed, and if by it is meant simply that any change in the status or policy of one part of the area is bound to have a profound effect on all others, then its validity is beyond dispute. If, however, it is meant to imply the existence of a system of checks and balances that automatically tends to counteract any attempt to alter the existing balance, the assumptions underlying such a view must be examined with some caution.

The Scandinavian balance, it is said, depends not only on preserving the existing situation but also on keeping alive certain options for changing it. Thus, it is believed that Soviet policy towards Finland is influenced not only by the fact that Sweden continues to adhere to neutrality but also by the possibility that a change of Soviet policy toward Finland might cause Sweden to abandon her neutrality. Similarly, it is claimed that Norway and Denmark help to maintain the balance by retaining their right to give up their self-imposed restraint on the stationing of foreign forces or nuclear weapons.

Such theories would make sense only if it is taken for granted that the Soviet Union has aggressive designs on Finland and is deterred from carrying them out by the fear of provoking the other Scandinavian states into close military co-operation with the Western Powers. Yet a great deal of evidence can be presented in favour of the contention that Soviet policy towards Finland, or indeed towards Scandinavia as a whole, has been consistently defensive – and that it has been defensive not only after the founding of NATO but well before that time: in 1944 the Soviet Union settled with Finland on terms that preserved Finnish independence; in 1945 it did nothing to disturb the free parliamentary elections held in Finland, and it voluntarily withdrew its forces from the Danish island of Bornholm and the Northern province of Norway, the two Scandinavian areas it had occupied as part of the operations against Germany; in 1948 it accepted the Finnish draft for a treaty that confirmed Finland's desire to stay neutral; and in 1955 it agreed to evacuate its naval base at Porkkala.

Once it is assumed that Soviet policy, in a military sense, is defensive rather than aggressive, then the 'Scandinavian options' look different – provocative rather than deterrent, and likely to feed the suspicions of the Russian mind. It would then follow, too, that Finnish policy must work towards removing the uncertainties about Scandinavian intentions. For it is of course a paramount Finnish interest, as President Kekkonen has pointed out, to do whatever can be done to avert the kind of situation that might trigger the defence mechanism provided by the Finnish-Soviet Treaty of 1948.

Kekkonen has not concealed his view that in this sense the ideal would be a neutral Scandinavia. As early as in November 1954, when he was still Prime Minister, Kekkonen pointed out that since an attack 'against the Soviet Union through Finland' – the key phrase of the treaty – could be carried out physically only through the territories of the other Scandinavian states, the creation of a neutral Scandinavian bloc would serve to remove even a theoretical threat of such an attack.[1]

In the 1950s a European conflict on the conventional pattern of the Second World War was still discussed as a real possibility that had to be taken into account in the framing of security policies. In the 1960s this danger was replaced by the threat of a further spread of nuclear weapons as the principal source of international insecurity and tension. President Kekkonen accordingly shifted his attention to the implications of this problem for the Scandinavian area.

The lessons of the Cuban missile crisis seemed to be particularly relevant. Cuba is sometimes compared with Finland, but actually just about everything about Finland today is different from the Cuban situation. Finland has not defied the security interests of her powerful neighbour by permitting the establishment of hostile missile bases on her soil or proclaimed a campaign to subvert the

Communist regimes in Eastern Europe; nor, for that matter, has the Soviet Union attempted to overthrow the Finnish regime by military means. Nevertheless, the missile crisis carried a powerful message, for Finland as well for all small countries. It revealed the explosive political consequences of any change in the nuclear arms balance. It could be argued, and Defence Secretary Robert McNamara did make the point, that since the Soviet Union already had the capability of firing missiles at the United States from its own territory or from nuclear-powered submaries, from a purely military point of view the existence of Soviet missile bases in Cuba would not have materially altered the military balance of power between the two countries. Yet psychologically – that is, politically – the introduction of Soviet nuclear weapons into the immediate vicinity of the American mainland was judged to be intolerable. The American reaction to the presence of Soviet missiles in Cuba makes it easier to understand Soviet sensitivity to any possible increase of NATO activity in Norway and Denmark.

A few months later, in April 1963, the Swedish Government pointed out that the Cuban crisis had been 'an object lesson' of the continued relevance of what had become known as the 'Undén Plan'. Sweden's former Foreign Minister Östen Undén, in November 1961, had introduced the concept of nuclear-free zones into the disarmament negotiations as one possible means by which the spread of nuclear weapons could be prevented. According to his suggestion countries forming such zones might enter into mutual undertakings to refrain from manufacturing or otherwise acquiring nuclear weapons and to refuse to receive such weapons on their territory on behalf of any other country. The Undén Plan was put forward in general terms without reference to any particular geographical area, and the Swedish Government itself insisted that before countries without nuclear weapons could be expected to forego the right to acquire them the nuclear powers would have to take steps to limit the nuclear arms race, in the first place by agreeing on the banning of all nuclear tests.

But in the spring of 1963 the negotiations on a test ban were making no progress, and international tension was mounting. In the beginning of May the Secretary-General of the United Nations, U Thant, suggested that efforts to create nuclear-free zones should be pursued without waiting for a test ban. He made this statement during a visit to Yugoslavia, and by coincidence President Kekkonen, too, was at the time among President Tito's guests. The two did not actually meet in Yugoslavia, but U Thant's statement made a strong impression on Kekkonen, and soon after his return to Finland he acted along the lines the Secretary-General had suggested.

In an interview with the London *Times* on 28th May 1963, the Finnish President said that the question of the control of nuclear weapons had become the central issue in international politics. Small countries could do little to solve it: the nuclear powers themselves had the main responsibility. But even small countries could contribute to a peaceful solution, and the least they could do was to refrain from doing anything that might increase tension. Kekkonen went on to recall the Undén Plan and U Thant's statement and pointed out that the Cuban missile crisis had demonstrated that any move to place nuclear weapons into areas where none had been before, or under the control of countries that had not had such weapons, would inevitably create great tension and insecurity. For obvious reasons the area he was primarily concerned about was Scandinavia. Finland was already committed by her Peace Treaty to refrain from acquiring nuclear weapons, and the Finnish Government had made it clear that in accordance with its policy of neutrality it would refuse to receive such weapons on its territory on behalf of any other power. None of the other Scandinavian countries had nuclear weapons on their territories. Thus Scandinavia in fact constituted a nuclear-free zone. But Kekkonen pointed out that this depended on the unilateral, national policies of each of the four countries and suggested that the nuclear-free status of Scandinavia be confirmed through mutual undertakings in the manner outlined in the Undén Plan. Since such an arrangement would only formalize the existing state of affairs, he argued, it could not be said to change the international balance of power or damage the security interests of any outside power. For the Scandinavian states themselves, he said, it would mean greater security and stability by removing them unequivocally from the 'the realm of nuclear speculation'.[2]

The 'Kekkonen Plan' followed the new logic of the nuclear age in which increased military power does not necessarily enhance national security. According to conventional logic it would seem that both the deterrent effect and the defensive capability of a nation's armed forces would be improved through acquisition of the most effective weapons available. Thus, in Sweden as well as in Denmark and Norway it has been argued that small nations need tactical nuclear arms so as to have the means to force a superior enemy to disperse his forces. The fallacy of this line of reasoning has been exposed by Östen Undén, among others, in a little book[3] he published after his retirement in 1963. He points out that the advocates of tactical nuclear arms seem to envisage a conventional large-scale invasion of Sweden – the type of attack least likely to occur. The real danger to Swedish security – and what Undén says about Sweden is equally applicable to Finland – is not a separate, local aggression, but involuntary involvement in a general European conflict. Possession of nuclear weapons would not be an asset in any effort to avoid that danger. It would more likely be a hazard. For instead of deterring a potential aggressor it might well attract a preventive strike from one of the nuclear powers. To plead that tactical nuclear weapons are defensive would not necessarily save the country in such a situation. For the difference between tactical and strategic, defensive and offensive, cannot be objectively determined. It depends on a subjective judgement about the intentions of the country possessing the weapons. And in the heat of a supreme crisis governments are notoriously apt to misjudge each other's intentions. Undén concluded that since there was no defence against nuclear attack it was 'more important to limit the danger of being involved in war than to strengthen military capabilities': this was also the essence of the Kekkonen Plan.

Kekkonen's reasoning received striking support in the report on the effects of the possible use of nuclear weapons prepared by twelve eminent authorities representing as many countries, including all the nuclear powers, and issued in October 1967 by the Secretary-General of the United Nations. 'Having nuclear weapons on one's own territory', the report stated, 'might bring with it the penalty of becoming a direct target for nuclear attack.' Another conclusion of special relevance to Scandinavia was that 'the acquisition by any nation of nuclear weapons could also trigger a change in its international relations'. Moreover, the report persuasively argued that the difference between tactical and strategic nuclear weapons was largely illusory: 'Given that both sides to a conflict deploy nuclear weapons, it is highly debatable whether there are any circumstances of land warfare in which such weapons could be used as battlefield weapons or, if they were so used, would confer any military advantage to either side in the zone of contact.'[4]

The intellectual force of the arguments that could be deployed in favour of the Kekkonen Plan could not, however, overcome the power of the political realities that determined the reaction of the other Scandinavian states. In Sweden, a national consensus on defence policies depended on agreement to postpone any decision on whether or not to acquire nuclear weapons, and the Government was unwilling to do anything to upset it. For Denmark and Norway, acceptance of the Kekkonen Plan would have meant virtual exclusion from the NATO defence system; it would also have caused acute political embarrassment to their allies. Besides, in all three countries, while there was considerable support for the idea of contracting out of the nuclear arms race, probably majority opinion favoured keeping the nuclear option open. Consequently each of the three governments responded to Kekkonen's suggestion with a re-statement of its established policy on nuclear arms, but went no further. At a meeting of the Scandinavian foreign ministers in Stockholm in September 1963 the Kekkonen Plan was discussed but, owing to Norwegian opposition, no reference to it was made in the customary communiqué issued after the meeting. The Norwegian position was that its nuclear policy was exclusively its own concern and not subject to discussion within the Scandinavian group. Yet about a year later, in July 1964, during Nikita Khruschev's visit to Denmark and Norway, both Scandinavian governments agreed to joint communiqués in which the Soviet Government expressed its appreciation for the refusal of Denmark and Norway to permit the stationing of nuclear weapons on their territories. The usual reservation that this applied only in peace-time was omitted. These statements, Kekkonen was quick to point out, served in practice the same purpose as his plan for a nuclear-free Scandinavia.[5]

Nevertheless Kekkonen's various Scandinavian initiatives have aroused not only opposition and criticism but even irritation and resentment in the other Scandinavian countries, particularly of course in Denmark and Norway. He has been accused of meddling in the affairs of others or, worse still, promoting the Soviet cause at the expense of the security of Finland's western neighbours. To a great extent the differences between Kekkonen and his Scandinavian critics can be traced back to the difference in their respective assessments of Soviet policy. If it is assumed that the Soviet Union is contemplating the possibility of launching a military aggression against Finland and the rest of Scandinavia, then Kekkonen's suggestions may indeed appear suspect. But if one accepts his contention, based on more than twenty years' experience of dealing with Finnish-Soviet relations, that Soviet policy is essentially defensive but is apt to react, or even over-react, to any indication of increased Western, particularly West German, military activity in the area, then his ideas can be seen to reflect what is clearly in the interest of Finland. Indeed, his statements on Scandinavian affairs have been primarily statements on Finnish policy and only secondarily proposals addressed to others, though often the real contents have got lost with the wrapping. When, in 1954, Kekkonen spoke of a neutral Scandinavia, he introduced under that cover for the first time the idea of a neutral Finland into public discussion. And when, in November 1965, he spoke about a treaty to ensure that the Finnish-Norwegian border in Lapland would remain peaceful in a conflict between NATO and the Warsaw Pact, he thereby emphasized the defensive character of the Finnish commitments under the Finnish-Soviet Treaty of 1948 and sought to remove Norwegian fears that Finnish Lapland might be used as a staging area for Soviet aggressive action against Norway.

The debate on the future security policies of the Scandinavian states is bound to gain in intensity with the approach of April 1969, the date after which member states of the North Atlantic Alliance can withdraw at one year's notice. Once again the idea of a Scandinavian defence pact is being discussed. It failed to materialize in the 1930s, for reasons dealt with in a previous chapter. In 1948–49, the possibility of creating a Scandinavian alliance was discussed between Denmark, Norway and Sweden – without Finland. Again, nothing came of it, for reasons that lie outside the scope of this book. The failure of the talks was termed a blow to Scandinavian unity, for as a result Denmark and Norway joined NATO, while Sweden remained neutral. But for Finland it was fortunate, and in the long run the failure in 1949 probably saved the future of Scandinavian co-operation in the wider sense which must include Finland. The emergence of a defence alliance between Denmark, Norway and Sweden would have isolated Finland and made it more difficult for her to join in the process of integration that has taken place in the area. As it was, Finland waited until the favourable international winds of 1955 before joining the Nordic Council, the consultative organ of co-operation of the parliaments of its members, which does not deal with matters of defence. Since then the full participation of

Finland in Scandinavian co-operation has been taken for granted. Proceeding pragmatically, without a federalist programme, the Scandinavian nations have gradually achieved a greater degree of integration than probably any other group of sovereign states. They have created a passport union, a common labour market, and an integrated system of social security; they continue to extend co-ordination of legislation to an ever-widening sphere of human activity; and since the beginning of 1968 they have eliminated tariff barriers on manufactured goods. The claim that today Finns, Danes, Norwegians and Swedes are citizens of Scandinavia as well as of their own states is more than a catch-phrase.

It is tempting to project the unity and solidarity achieved in so many fields to the area of defence. The war-time experiences that pulled Scandinavia apart in 1948 and 1949 are receding into history. The motives and arguments of twenty years ago have lost much of their reality. At that time the Norwegians and Danes – particularly the Norwegians – were determined not to be caught once again, as they had been in April 1940, unprepared and unprotected. They had lost their faith in neutrality. They believed the Soviet Union presented an immediate military menace and they were convinced that only the combined defensive power of the Western world, including the United States, could deter a Soviet aggression. At the end of the 1960s the world scene looks very different. The Soviet Union today appears in the role of a conservative power, preoccupied with internal development, profoundly disturbed about China, anxious to keep things in Europe as they are; the United States, deeply involved in Asian affairs, is co-operating with the Soviet Union to prevent the spread of nuclear weapons and thus to keep West Germany in its place. The Cold War is already being written about as history. True, the Soviet intervention in Czechoslovakia in August 1968 was a setback to the trend of closer co-operation between East and West in Europe. Yet it did not change the structure of the European situation. It only showed to what lengths the Soviet Union was prepared to go to maintain the *status quo*.

In Finland, the idea of a Scandinavian defence community seems attractive to some sections of opinion. It is hoped that the Soviet Union might be willing to trade its security treaty with Finland for the exit of Denmark and Norway from NATO. But the Finnish-Soviet Treaty of 1948 is not commensurable with Danish and Norwegian membership in NATO. It is not a treaty of alliance. It has not prevented Finland from developing a policy of neutrality recognized as such by all the great powers. Indeed, it is a fallacy to imagine that the position of Finland would materially change if the treaty ceased to be in force. For the provisions of the treaty are descriptive as much as they are normative: they state what will actually happen, treaty or no treaty, in certain precisely defined circumstances. As the European situation has become more stable and peaceful, the likelihood that these circumstances might arise has steadily diminished, but the purpose of Finnish policy must continue to be to prevent their occurring rather than to abolish the treaty – to remove any possible causes of fever rather than to throw away the thermometer.

This purpose is hardly served by a Scandinavian defence alliance, nor does such an alliance seem relevant to the real needs of Scandinavia as a whole in the foreseeable future. A defence alliance is a means to an end, which normally is to increase the security of its members in the face of a common enemy. Who might be the common enemy of the Scandinavian states today? Or would their alliance be designed to provide a defence against all comers, including the Soviet Union and the United States? To mention the thought is to dismiss it. For the real threat to Scandinavian security no longer comes from this or that power or combination of powers: it arises from situations and events that are difficult to foresee with any precision. The enemy no longer can be identified by his uniform or flag: it is the spectre of war itself. It is the danger that even a distant conflict, or a crisis in no way connected with Scandinavian interests, may spark a general war that engulfs the innocent bystander. In the face of this enemy, the historical and geographical factors that have divided Scandinavia are superseded by the overriding common interest in the preservation of international peace and security. But the conclusion to be drawn from this analysis is not that Scandinavia needs a common military defence but, rather, more intensive and effective political co-operation in international affairs.

Such co-operation is already established practice. The Foreign Ministers of the Scandinavian countries meet regularly twice a year to exchange views and information on the international situation and to co-ordinate policies in the United Nations. Apart from these more formal meetings, the Foreign Ministries consult each other informally and at all levels continuously, and Scandinavian missions and representatives abroad always maintain close contact. All this is done, not on the basis of agreements or according to prescribed procedures, but as a matter of course: it is a habit rather than a system. Such intimate co-operation in matters of foreign policy between five countries of which three belong to a military alliance and two are neutral, is in itself not only a remarkable expression of the unity of outlook and interest between them but also a practical contribution to the lessening of international tension and strengthening of peace in Europe. As the various security arrangements made in different historical circumstances tend to lose immediate relevancy, the factors separating the Scandinavian countries are receding into the background, and the common outlook and interest, and the co-operation based on them, gain in importance. Even more significant perhaps than the co-operation between the Scandinavian foreign ministers is the fact that since 1967 even the defence ministers of Denmark, Finland, Norway and Sweden have instituted regular annual meetings. True, they do not discuss the defence policies of their countries in the usual sense of the term; they deal exclusively with matters relating to Scandinavian preparations for, and participation in, United Nations peace-keeping operations (a subject discussed more fully in the next chapter). But it may well be that in the long run this kind of military co-operation, which is designed to help in the maintenance of international peace in general rather than directly in the defence of the Scandinavian area itself, will be recognized as the primary means for safeguarding the security of the four countries.

XI. *Keeping the Peace*

ON FINLAND'S FIFTIETH ANNIVERSARY OF INDEPENDENCE, in December 1967, Secretary-General U Thant sent President Kekkonen a message of congratulations in which he called Finland 'a model member of the United Nations'. There is no need to doubt the sincerity of the compliment. The Secretary-General has come to rely on a relatively small number of United Nations members to support the Organization beyond the call of duty, as it were, with money and police forces and other services, and Finland is one of them.

Today this is taken for granted. Yet not so long ago membership of the United Nations was regarded in Finland with serious misgivings. Although Finland had applied for membership in 1947, soon after ratification of the Peace Treaty, her admission was delayed by eight years, while the Great Powers argued and bargained on general admission policy. Of all the nations kept waiting, Finland was probably the least impatient, and when the dispute was finally resolved, and sixteen new members were admitted in December 1955, the reaction in Finland was far from enthusiastic. The United Nations at the time was regarded primarily as a battlefield of the Cold War. It was feared that Finland's policy of keeping out of trouble and controversy might be too severely tested through exposure to the conflicting pressures that were buffeting the Organization.

The very first General Assembly session in which Finland took part in the autumn of 1956 seemed to prove that the country would have been better off outside, quietly minding its own business. It was the session that dealt with the Hungarian crisis. For Finland, the issue presented a tragic dilemma. The emotions of the Finnish people, who regarded the Hungarians as their kin, were deeply engaged. The Government was urged by a strong opinion to express these emotions in New York. The Finnish delegation did state in the debate the hope that 'Hungary and the Soviet Union would be able to agree on the withdrawal of Soviet troops from Hungary and the safeguarding of the fundamental rights of the Hungarian people in a way that would correspond to their traditions of freedom.' But it abstained from voting on the resolutions condemning the Soviet action and demanding the withdrawal of Soviet troops. The abstentions were widely and indignantly criticized in Finland. It was not the first time that popular sentiment had come into conflict with a more tough-minded view of the national interest. On the Hungarian issue the Finnish Government had put good relations with the country's powerful neighbour before the luxury of making an emotionally satisfying gesture in the United Nations. It could also argue that a Finnish vote to condemn the Soviet Union, though it might have eased the conscience of the Finnish people, would have achieved nothing in the way of helping the Hungarians. Many Finns remembered what had happened in the League of Nations in December 1939 when Finland had been invaded. The Finnish Government had appealed to the League in the hope of resuming negotiations with the Soviet Government. It was in vain. In the end the League by majority vote declared the Soviet Union guilty of aggression and expelled it. But the vote revealed the depressing fact that the courage of member nations, as expressed in their willingness to punish the Soviet Union through sanctions or render assistance to Finland, was in direct proportion to their distance from the scene of action. The end result helped Finland neither to make peace nor to defend herself.

While the Hungarian crisis was tearing the Assembly apart, the parallel crisis of Suez provided an example of novel and imaginative ways of using the Organization for containing an international conflict and keeping the peace. It also provided Finland with an opportunity to play a positive and active role on the international scene. Secretary-General Dag Hammarskjöld needed a military adviser to organize the United Nations Emergency Force and he asked for a Finnish general. He also asked Finland, along with the other Scandinavian states, for troops for peace-keeping in the Middle East. The Finnish Government readily agreed. By helping the United Nations Finland was helping herself: her participation in the United Nations peace-keeping mission traced the first outline of a new image of Finland as a nation with an independent position outside military blocs and trusted by all concerned, Arabs and Israel, Russians and Americans, to carry out her self-assumed duties impartially and effectively.

Indeed, it did not take long for Finland to overcome the doubts and inhibitions that had marked her entry into the United Nations. As President Kekkonen pointed out in November 1962, Finland's participation in the activities of the United Nations, far from causing harm to her interests, had in fact helped to consolidate Finland's policy of neutrality and to gain international recognition for it. A great deal has happened since 1956. For one thing, Finland now faces the world with greater self-confidence. But the world, too, has changed and the United Nations with it. The Organization now provides neutral countries like Finland with a more congenial political environment. The new states of Africa and Asia, which have doubled the membership of the Organization since Finland's entry, are impatient with the stale issues of the Cold War. They look upon the United Nations primarily as an instrument for helping the peoples still living under colonial rule to achieve independence, for combating racial inequality, and for promoting the economic development of the poor and hungry and illiterate majority of the world population. The focus of United Nations interest and attention has shifted away from East-West issues towards the problems of the new North-South confrontation. International tension no longer emanates from Europe but rather from the political and economic turbulence in the Third World, and in particular from the uncertainties and anxieties caused by the great unknown – Mao's China.

For the functioning of the United Nations the changing relationship between the United States and the Soviet Union has had a decisive importance. The dual crisis of 1956 had made this brutally plain. On Hungary, the Soviet Union and the United States could not be reconciled and the United Nations Assembly session was reduced to a battle of angry words. On Suez, Soviet and American interests coincided and the United Nations could be effectively employed to contain the conflict. The lesson was clear. The United Nations can be made to serve its primary purpose of maintaining international peace and security only in the event that there exists at least a minimum measure of agreement and co-operation between the leading powers – and today there are only two powers that really matter. Any attempt to make use of the United Nations on the vital issues of international life on a different basis would be tantamount to transforming the Organization into an alliance for the purpose of imposing the will of one group of nations upon another, and no such attempt could succeed without destroying the United Nations in the process: the controversy over the Congo operation almost did destroy it.

Through most of the 1960s, though perhaps not until after the Cuban crisis, the United Nations has been able to function on the basis of that necessary minimum measure of agreement between the superpowers. Despite their irreconcilable differences on many fundamental issues of international life and their fierce rivalry for influence among the nations of the world, the United States and the Soviet Union have in fact found it possible to use the United Nations as an instrument of co-operation, not so much for the purpose of settling problems affecting their own vital interests as to preventing such peripheral crises and conflicts as Kashmir, Cyprus and the Middle East from endangering world peace.

Yet the power of the two giants, though decisive, is neither absolute nor exclusive in shaping the influence of the United Nations on the course of international developments. For today not even the most powerful nations can remain unaffected by the constant flow of consultation, the continuing process of collective negotiations, the never-ending effort to reconcile and adjust differing views and interests, the insistent search for an international consensus which goes on in the United Nations and in which neutral countries can play a useful role. It is the cumulative effect of this process itself, rather than its superficial results in any given situation, that exerts a growing influence on the behaviour of states, compelling as it does governments preoccupied with domestic affairs to take into account, to some extent at least, the seamless interdependence of all nations and the constant interaction between their policies. It is an influence difficult to measure, almost imperceptible to a contemporary observer, like the slow erosion or gradual new growths caused by climatic changes. It is none the less an influence that is likely to pervade international relations to an ever-growing extent.

The real substance of the co-operation that takes place within the United Nations is largely hidden from view by the façade of dreary and often misleading public debate, the meaningless votes, and the inflated language of resolutions adopted. The dichotomy between words and deeds is usually a simple one: much talk against little or no action. But sometimes it is more complex. The vital issue of peace-keeping is a case in point. Judging by the debate that continues year after year it would seem that member states, and particularly the Great Powers, are irreconcilably divided on the relative competence of the Security Council and General Assembly as well as on the extent of the executive authority of the Secretary-General. But the debate is really about the past: it is about the Congo operation; and neither side is prepared to yield on the rights and wrongs of what has happened. In practice, however, United Nations intervention in the shape of police forces or observers or other types of 'presence' has become generally accepted as an indispensable tool available to the international community for use in crises and conflicts. In spite of the continuing differences on the constitutional principles involved, the Organization has in fact been able to provide such peace-keeping services as have been required by member nations. At the height of the constitutional crisis in the spring of 1964, the Security Council unanimously approved a major peace-keeping operation in Cyprus; in the following year it intervened in the Kashmir dispute; in June 1967, only a few weeks after the withdrawal of the United Nations Emergency Force from the Sinai desert, it discovered it urgently needed more United Nations observers to supervise the cease-fire between Israel and her Arab neighbours. Significantly all these operations have been initiated by unanimous decision of the Security Council: they all reflect the necessary measure of basic agreement between the Great Powers. In the Finnish view, as it has been expressed in the General Assembly debates, practical political considerations, rather than constitutional theory, require that peace-keeping operations have the widest possible backing of the member states, including that of the Great Powers.

Ever since her first venture into the Middle East, Finland has contributed men or money to all United Nations peace-keeping undertakings – in most cases both men *and* money. Finnish officers have served or are serving as observers in the Lebanon, in Kashmir, and in Suez; a Finnish battalion is part of the United Nations force in Cyprus which is commanded by a Finnish general; Finland has provided a United Nations 'presence' for Laos and a mediator for the Cyprus dispute; Finland was among the first in 1962 to buy United Nations bonds, and again in 1965 to make a voluntary contribution, to help the Organization to overcome the financial difficulties caused by the dispute over paying for peace-keeping operations. In order to be able to respond promptly and efficiently to a United

Nations request for its services, Finland in close co-operation with the other Scandinavian states has set up stand-by forces, a kind of international voluntary fire-brigade, whose members are trained and otherwise prepared to take off at short notice for peace-keeping missions.

Thus the image of Finland first outlined in the Sinai desert in 1956 has been filled in and firmly impressed upon the world. The frequent and extensive use of Finnish services for United Nations peace-keeping and peace-making purposes is an indication of international recognition of Finland's neutrality and this in turn tends to strengthen respect for it: neutrality is a strange beast that feeds upon its own reflection. But Finland's commitment to the cause of United Nations peace-keeping goes beyond image-making. It stems from the understanding that it is in Finland's own interest to do whatever can be done to strengthen the peace-keeping capabilities of the United Nations as 'a rational and civilized method' – as U Thant has described it – for containing and ending conflicts and thus facilitating the peaceful settlement of international disputes. Clearly anything that is likely to ease international tension and reduce the risks of a general conflict is bound to serve the security of Finland. In the summer of 1939 Finnish students and schoolboys volunteered to dig trenches along the country's eastern border; today the men who volunteer to go to Cyprus to keep the peace (though their motives are probably pecuniary rather than patriotic) may be doing as much for Finland's security.

What has been said here of Finland's dedication to United Nations peace-keeping applies equally to the other Scandinavian countries. It would indeed be misleading to discuss Finland's role in the United Nations outside its Scandinavian context. In the United Nations, the differences between the security policies of the Scandinavian states have little relevance: their common Scandinavian identity takes precedence over the separate political characteristics of each. Co-operation between them is probably more intensive than between members of any other group of states, and in ninety-nine cases out of a hundred they find themselves reaching agreement without really trying. There is, one might say, a common Scandinavian outlook on international affairs that transcends differences of national policy – a rational, moderate, pragmatic approach well suited to the role of mediation so often assigned to Scandinavians. It could not very well be otherwise, for the Scandinavian nations have indeed every advantage: they are politically stable, socially advanced, economically prosperous; they have no major international claims to press or to counter; no present or recent colonial record, and no racial problems. In short, they have no good reason to behave in a fanatical, neurotic or irrational manner. They have every reason, in their own interest, to work for the still distant goal of a world order based on the United Nations Charter. The Scandinavian nations have consistently argued that the United Nations, to be effective, must become a universal organization; accordingly they support the admission of the People's Republic of China which they have all recognized. They are actively engaged in the search for a peaceful solution to the potentially explosive issues of Southern Africa. They are among the leading contributors to United Nations programme of economic assistance to under-developed countries.

The Finnish style in the United Nations reflects the national character. Finland's contribution to the output of words in the United Nations, for instance, has been mercifully modest. Finns tend to be the opposite of flamboyant, distrustful of rhetoric, interested in practical things rather than theory; they are also inclined to be withdrawn, even self-effacing, at worst isolationist and suspicious and intolerant of other, different peoples. But in the United Nations Finland is acquiring a new identity. Having been long convinced that their country is poor and their nation young, Finns now discover that less than one-third of the member states of the United Nations have achieved their sovereignty earlier and that according to statistics on *per capita* national income Finland is among the fifteen wealthiest nations in the world. They also discover that their country, by virtue of its neutrality and its friendly relations with all the Great Powers, can play a meaningful part in international efforts for peace and security.

XII. *No Cause for Pity*

AT THE YALTA CONFERENCE IN FEBRUARY 1945, THE BIG
Three believed they were in agreement on the principles that should
govern the reconstruction of Eastern and Central Europe after the
defeat of the Nazis. Roosevelt and Churchill recognized that the
Soviet Union was entitled, in the name of its security, to make sure
that the governments to be installed along Russia's borders would be
'friendly' to the Soviet Union. Stalin agreed with the Western
leaders that these governments must be 'independent and democratic'. The profound misunderstanding that lay behind these words
was revealed within weeks of the conference. In Western eyes, Yalta
meant free elections and parliamentary democracy, and as the Communists took over power in one Eastern European country after the
other, Stalin was accused of cynically betraying his solemn pledge.
To the Soviet Government, Yalta meant primarily security, and it
resented every Western attempt to influence political developments
in the area. The bitter arguments about what had in fact been agreed
in Yalta were the beginning of the Cold War.

In one country only have post-war political developments con-
formed, in a manner acceptable to both sides, to the pattern envis-
aged at Yalta. Finland has consistently pursued a policy that has
satisfied the Soviet craving for security. Finland has also maintained
her independence and parliamentary democracy in the sense that the
Western Powers understood these terms. Finland is friendly to the
Soviet Union without being subservient; she is a Western democracy without challenging Soviet security. As a consequence Finland
has hardly ever, in the quarter century that has passed since the
Yalta conference, even been mentioned in the disputes and quarrels
between East and West: the Cold War has passed her by.

This does not mean that Finland would have consciously adapted
herself to the Yalta agreement. It means, rather, that the Yalta

agreement reflected the realities of the Finnish situation, rather than those prevailing in the rest of Eastern and Central Europe. Unlike the other nations discussed at Yalta, the Finns had retained their independence throughout the Second World War. Finland had not been occupied by Germany and she was not occupied by the Soviet Union, nor was she subjected to unconditional surrender. Her parliamentary system never ceased to function: the first post-war election was held as early as in April 1945. Thus Finland at the time of the Yalta conference was in fact an independent, democratic nation. Independence did not have to be restored to Finland by the victorious powers; parliamentary democracy did not have to be introduced from the outside.

Equally important was that the Finns pursued with rigorous consistency a policy which, in the sense of the Yalta agreement, was friendly to the Soviet Union – not because the Big Three had so decreed, but because the Finns themselves, even before the Yalta conference, had decided that such a policy was in their best national interest. Consistency of purpose has been matched by flexibility of approach. Finland's foreign policy, as it has been described in preceding chapters, cannot be fitted into any conventional pattern. It has turned a mutual assistance pact with a great power into a prop for neutrality. It has employed the concept of diplomatic non-recognition as a means for widening the scope of international relations. It has succeeded in changing a treaty without revising it. At all times substance has been given precedence over appearance. In assessing the success of this policy, only results count, and the results are there for everyone to judge for himself. Today Finland is no longer the tragic hero of the Western world – a nation, as a British journalist once put it, 'much admired, often pitied, never envied'.[1] There is today perhaps not so much to admire. But there is no cause for pity. And for some peoples, there may be something to envy.

Notes

In addition to the published sources referred to in these Notes, I have been able to use, with the permission of the Ministry of Foreign Affairs of Finland, some information that has not been made public before. I am not permitted, however, to cite the documents or other sources from which such information has been obtained.

CHAPTER I.
1. *Memoirs*, by George Kennan (Little, Brown & Co., 1968), pp. 322-3.

CHAPTER II.
1. 'The Foreign Policy Attitudes of the Finns during the Swedish Rule', by Pentti Renvall, an article in *Finnish Foreign Policy*, published by the Finnish Political Science Association in 1963.
2. 'Finland's Foreign Policy as an Autonomous Grand Duchy' in *Finnish Foreign Policy*.
3. *The Victors in World War I and Finland*, by Juhani Paasivirta, published by the Finnish Historical Society, 1965.
4. See, for instance, *A History of Finland*, by John H. Wuorinen (Columbia University Press, 1965), pp. 22-53.
5. Text in Appendix B in Wuorinen, op. cit.
6. Wuorinen, op. cit., pp. 293-300.
7. This account of the background to, and the course of, the Finnish-Soviet conflict in 1939, up to page 30, is based on *The Diplomacy of the Winter War*, by Max Jakobson (Harvard University Press, 1961).
8. A full account of Finnish-German relations in 1940-41 based largely on German documents can be found in *Suomen Valinta 1941*, by Hans Peter Krosby, Helsinki, 1967 (to be published in English by Wisconsin University Press).
9. *The Memoirs of Marshal Mannerheim* (Cassell and Co. Ltd., 1953), pp. 415-60. Also *Finland and the Great Powers*, by G. A. Gripenberg (University of Nebraska Press, 1965), pp. 265 ff.

CHAPTER III.

1. *Making the Peace Treaties 1941-1947*. Publication of the Department of State, 1947, p. 77.
2. Gripenberg, op. cit., p. 201.
3. *Helsingin Sanomat*, 1st August 1946.
4. Enckell's speech in full in *Helsingin Sanomat*, 16th August 1946.
5. 'Finland's War Reparation Deliveries to the Soviet Union', by Jaakko Auer. (Article in *Finnish Foreign Policy*.)
6. *British Foreign Policy in the Second World War*, by Sir Llewellyn Woodward (H.M. Stationery Office, 1962), pp. 159-60, 296.
7. *Treaties of Peace*. U.S. Government Printing Office, Washington, D.C., 1947. Dept of State publication 2743, European Series 21.
8. *Urho Kekkonen. Puheita ja kirjoituksia. I* (Weilin & Göös, Helsinki, 1967), p. 122.

CHAPTER IV.

1. *The Second World War*, Volume I, by Winston Churchill (Cassell & Co. Ltd., 1948), pp. 250-1.
2. Text of the letter in *Paasikivi peräsimessä* by Toivo Heikkilä (Otava, 1965), p. 306.
3. Woodward, op. cit., p. 195.
4. *Dagens Nyheter*, 12th February 1947.
5. Text of Treaty in *Introduction to Finland 1960*, pp. 109-10.
6. Text of statement in *Helsingin Sanomat* of 10th April 1948.

CHAPTER V.

1. Text of statements on Kekkonen's talks with Macmillan and Kennedy in *Ulkopoliittisia lausuntoja ja asiakirjoja 1961* (an annual publication of Finland's Foreign Ministry henceforth referred to as *UAL*), pp. 109 and 129. Statement by de Gaulle in *UAL* 1962, p. 102.
2. *UAL* 1963, p. 15.
3. *Tankar om utrikespolitik*, by Östen Undén. (Raben & Sjögren, Stockholm, 1963.)
4. *UAL*, 1961, p. 134.

CHAPTER VI.

1. *UAL* 1962, p. 22.
2. *UAL* 1959, pp. 81-2.
3. *Urho Kekkonen*, op. cit., pp. 333-4.
4. *Helsingin Sanomat*, 8th January 1968.

CHAPTER VII.

1. *Helsingin Sanomat*, 12th July 1947.
2. *UAL* 1959, pp. 45-54.

3. *UAL* 1959, pp. 60-73.
4. *UAL* 1960, pp. 101-4.
5. *UAL* 1960, pp. 112-16.
6. *UAL* 1961, pp. 203-6.
7. *The EFTA Reporter*, no. 170, 9th October 1967, p. 3.

CHAPTER VIII.
1. *A Thousand Days*, by Arthur M. Schlesinger, Jr. (Houghton Mifflin Company, Boston, 1965), p. 395.
2. Ibid. p. 374.
3. *UAL* 1961, pp. 209-13.
4. *UAL* 1961, pp. 132-3.
5. *UAL* 1961, p. 131.
6. *UAL* 1961, pp. 148-50.
7. *UAL* 1961, pp. 38-44.
8. *UAL* 1961, p. 178.
9. *UAL* 1961, pp. 179-81.
10. *UAL* 1961, pp. 183-4, 185-93.
11. *Strategy of Peace*, by John F. Kennedy (Harper & Row, 1960), p. 160.

CHAPTER IX.
1. *UAL* 1963, p. 45.
2. *UAL* 1965, pp. 31-8.

CHAPTER X
1. *Urho Kekkonen*, op. cit., pp. 239-42.
2. *UAL* 1963, pp. 28-9.
3. Undén, op. cit.
4. *Effects of the Possible Use of Nuclear Weapons and the Security and Economic Implications for States of the Acquisition and Further Development of these Weapons* (United Nations, 1968), pp. 31-8.
5. *UAL* 1964, p. 26.

CHAPTER XII.
1. Patrick O'Donovan in *The Observer*, 11th August, 1963.

Index